25 YEARS OF
TAGGART

25 YEARS OF TAGGART

Behind the scenes of TV's longest-running police drama

THOMAS QUINN

Foreword by Blythe Duff

headline

This book is published to celebrate 25 years of the television series *Taggart*,
made by SMG TV Productions

First published in 2007 by
HEADLINE PUBLISHING GROUP

1

Cataloguing in Publication Data is available from the British Library

ISBN 978 0 7553 1527 7

Design by Dan Newman

Printed and bound in France by
Pollina - n° L44070

Headline's policy is to use papers that are natural, renewable and recyclable products and made
from wood grown in sustainable forests. The logging and manufacturing processes are expected
to conform to the environmental regulations of the country of origin.

HEADLINE PUBLISHING GROUP
An Hachette Livre UK Company
338 Euston Road
London NW1 3BH

www.headline.co.uk
www.hodderheadline.com

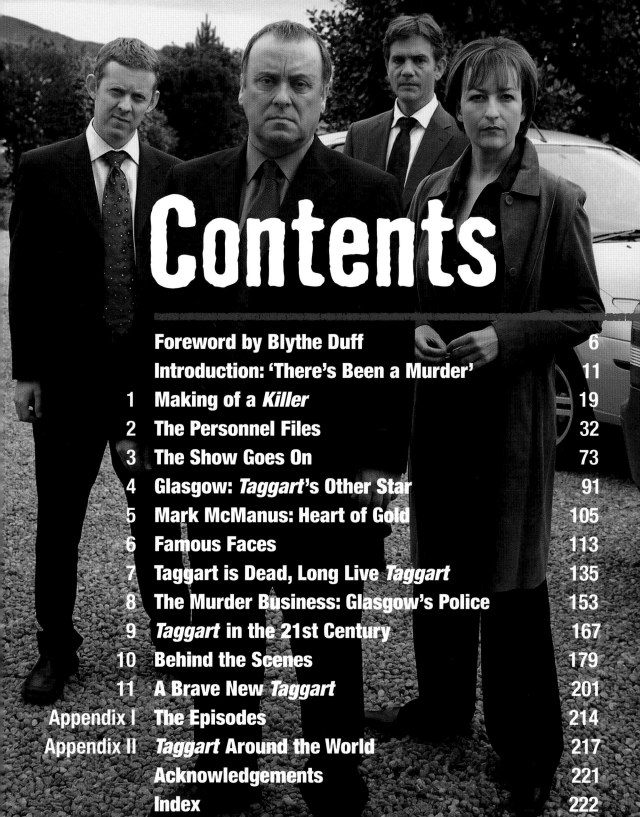

Contents

Foreword

by Blythe Duff

'I've heard this is the last *Taggart* ever,' someone said to me during my first *Taggart* experience, 'Death Comes Softly'. It was 1990 and I had just been cast as WPC Jackie Reid (nineteenth on the cast list in those days). If truth be told, I was just relieved *Taggart 15* had started filming at all. It had been postponed because Mark McManus – DCI Jim Taggart – had had to spend a week in hospital and I was rather selfishly worried that for the rest of my career I would have to tell people, 'No, I've never worked in television, although I was *almost* in a *Taggart* once!' It's hard to believe that we're now in our twenty-fifth year, will have completed ninety-three *Taggart* stories by the end of 2007, and hold the title of Britain's longest-running detective drama. And, a few promotions down the line, it's a dream come true that I'm *still* playing Jackie Reid.

If I had a pound for every time someone asked me why I think the series has stood the test of time, Jackie Reid would be able to take early retirement! The answer is that I don't know for sure, but it has a lot to do with the audience liking something they feel familiar with: the characters, the style, the black humour and the 'gritty' stories. You know what you are getting when you tune in and perhaps one very important point is that although the programme has gone through many changes during its time it remains true to its original intention: to be a good 'whodunit'.

The City of Glasgow has always played an important part, and not just for the ex-pats who love to be reminded of where their aunties or grannies grew up. More than that, it provides the scriptwriters with a wonderful backdrop against which to play out the often-macabre storylines. I was speaking to a journalist who had been watching the programme dubbed into French while on holiday. He mentioned to his French friends that this drama was set in his hometown of Glasgow. They were surprised it was Scotland, let alone Glasgow, which would suggest that not only does the programme 'travel' well – to over sixty countries in fact – but that the city itself has a cosmopolitan feel. The city has worked hard over the last few years to mix modern architecture with old. We have embraced the café culture (weather permitting!) and when filming on the rooftops the wonderful domes and spires are seen at their best, rivalling many European cities. Indeed *Taggart* has created a wonderful archive of Glasgow over the last twenty-five years, something that the City of Glasgow appreciates. In 2004 the programme was honoured with a dinner in the magnificent City Chambers and the cast and crew were presented with the Lord Provost's Special Award for Entertainment.

The following year the *Taggart* fan club arrived in Glasgow to establish the first ever convention. It was a special night and a perfect excuse for the original creator and executive producer of the series, Glenn Chandler and Robert Love, to celebrate with Eric Coulter (the current head of drama at programme maker's SMG) and Graeme Gordon (the current series producer). It provided a wonderful opportunity for the fans from all over the world to meet with each other, quiz the cast and share their enthusiasm for the programme.

Taggart is a £100 million pound business and has provided thousands of job opportunities in the film and television industry over the years. It has proved an amazing apprenticeship for hundreds of actors/technicians/script writers/producers – every field of the industry. It's a proud moment for the programme when we see someone who started as a runner return ten years later as a director.

One thing, which started in the Mark McManus era and continues today, is the 'non starry' atmosphere while working on set. The core company are always delighted to hear guest artists mention that there is such a 'relaxed' feeling on the show. It's a well-oiled machine and well served by all the departments, from the executive producer down. We like to enjoy ourselves. Humour is a very important aspect of the *Taggart* storylines, allowing the darker elements within the plot to come through. And filming on the streets of Glasgow has provided us with more than a few laughs over the years. There was the 'wee wummin' who inquired as to what we were filming, digested the answer, then replied, 'Och aye *Taggart*… is it a repeat?' And there was the lady who was furious we were filming in her street. If only she had known, she would have washed her windows! How about the suggestion from one fan that if the company needed a replacement for Mark McManus then they should look no further than Sir Alex Ferguson, Jim Taggart's spitting image. And I remember the teenage girls clutching their signed photos of James Macpherson while watching us film. They were so jealous of the fact that I was even breathing the same air as he was and asked one of the crew, 'Who is that lassie wae him?' Stuck for words, she answered that I was his 'helper'! They wittily replied, 'Oh aye… cow that she is!'

No matter where you go in Glasgow, someone will stop and tell you that we have filmed in their aunt's, their cousin's, or their neighbour's house. If another production company chooses to film in Glasgow they have to put up with the fact that every five minutes someone will ask them, 'What are you filming – is it *Taggart*?' Sometimes it's just easier to say 'yes'. And not one day passes without some wit shouting, 'There's been a murder!'

Three generations have now watched the programme. I was reminded of this when I was acting with a young eighteen-year-old actor recently. It dawned on me that I started in *Taggart* as he was being born, but he hadn't watched the programme for fourteen years of his life because his mum wouldn't let him! It delights us all to think of the millions of fans from all over the world who have watched the series throughout the years. Thank you all for your loyalty.

So when the wind is blowing around the camera departments' ears as we stand in the cloisters of Glasgow University… When the rain is horizontal and running down the production assistants' neck as we perch on an embankment on the Clyde… When the sound department has to contend with the noise from the flight path during the summer months… When the third assistant has to ask the kids outside Greggs the Bakers to slurp their soup more quietly… When the sparks have to stand in the middle of a midge-infested field or the caterers have to satisfy the tired and hungry when we should have called lunch at one… This book is for everyone who has contributed to the series over the years. We know we can do it, we know why we do it. Let's hope we continue to do it for as long as we can…

Here's tae us, wha's like us, gae few and they're aw deid!

Best wishes,

Blythe Duff
x

Introduction

'There's Been a Murder'

In 1982 Scottish Television's head of drama, Robert Love, spotted that ITV was short of a good detective series, so he commissioned a young writer, Glenn Chandler, to come up with one. The result was *Killer*, a three-part pilot for what was to become *Taggart*, the longest-running detective show in British television history.

It seems ironic now that Mark McManus's 1983 debut as Glasgow's toughest detective wasn't named after the character at all. *Killer* introduced Mark as Jim Taggart, a role he would play until his death in 1994. The drama was named after McManus's character from 1985, and *Taggart* has flourished under the same brand ever since.

Opposite: How many people does it take to film an episode of *Taggart*? Cast and crew in 1986 and twenty years later in 2006.

Above: McManus in *Taggart*'s three-part pilot episode, *Killer*.

At first, there was no guarantee this gritty whodunit written by Glenn Chandler, a relative television newcomer, would be granted a sequel, let alone a run of a quarter of a century. However, what was immediately apparent to everyone involved in the production, and to the millions at home who tuned in, was that they wanted to know *who did it*, and that in McManus, television had a new and highly original star. Leading men aren't supposed to look the way Mark did. He was short – too short for a policeman, as it happened – and he had a face that…well, to say it was lived in is an understatement. Jim Taggart's face looked like it had squatters.

He was an instant hit. But what was it about Jim Taggart that was new or different? His careworn expression and even his car coat might belong to David Jason's Frost. The hostile growl sounds a bit like John Thaw's irascible Morse. As for his weary sense of justice, well, that's Ian Rankin's creation Rebus, isn't it? Yes, but Jim Taggart predates all of these rival detectives while boasting a trait none of the others have really pulled off: a deliciously dark sense of humour.

In 1983 television was only beginning to wake up to the power of a bloody murder story and the emotive pull of a good detective. *The Sweeney* and *Z Cars* had put police work on the box – *The Bill* wouldn't make its debut for another year – but these were very different kinds of shows. Their plots revolved around police procedure or cops and robbers chases, or dwelled on the private lives of the characters. There were no screaming tyres and posing gangsters in *Killer*; this was a murder mystery of a style Agatha Christie would have recognised, yet set in the exotic gloom of contemporary Glasgow and with what at the time was a surprising taste for the gothic.

The success of *Taggart* over the years has relied on many different elements and many different people working both in front of the camera and behind it. But there is no denying the lift given to the *Taggart* brand by this first episode, by its powerful combination of a leading man at the height of his powers giving an enigmatic, unforgettable performance; plots that twisted and turned, gripping viewers; and an unusual, hard location that had been crying out for exposure on television.

You felt Jim Taggart wasn't just a Glasgow cop, but that he embodied the city itself: the tough underdog, quietly determined to succeed. From

Jim Taggart's face looked like it had squatters.

the off he is set apart from his Edinburgh-born sidekick, Livingstone, a middle-class graduate on a fast track to promotion within the police force, or, as Jim puts it with a growl, a 'flier'. By contrast, Taggart never had the chance to go to university. His father was a tram driver and he'd had to work his way up from the beat, each promotion hard-earned and, you imagine, most likely begrudged by his 'betters'. He summed up the city's view of itself completely.

'That was us, Taggart and Jardine'

As *Taggart* became one of the most popular television programmes of the 1980s, its hero softened a little. The feud with Livingstone came to an end when the actor Alastair Duncan – then called Neil Duncan – decided to try his luck elsewhere. Robert Love, now the programme's executive producer, recruited James Macpherson, a twenty-six-year-old actor from Mark McManus's home town of Hamilton. Detective Sergeant Michael Jardine, as he was in those days before rising through the ranks to detective chief inspector, was often guilty of the crime of being young and inexperienced,

There was to be no shortage of corpses for DS Jardine.

but the fact Jim Taggart had known his father meant they enjoyed a close bond from the beginning. Looking back on their on-screen partnership today, Macpherson sees it reflected in other shows, most notably in the BBC's *Dalziel and Pascoe*: 'Two men, one older, one younger, who generally get on pretty well. That was us, Taggart and Jardine.'

Jardine was a different sort of character to Jim Taggart. Although introduced as a teetotal Christian, these lifestyle choices were less important as the series went on, though he remained generally uptight – a bit too straight – and hopeless when it came to women.

With his blond hair and sculpted cheekbones, Macpherson was extremely popular with female viewers, yet McManus, far from being jealous that Macpherson might steal his limelight, actively encouraged his co-star and grew to rely on him. He was an extremely generous actor, but there were other reasons, too. The Glasgow-based independent television company STV always loyally defended its star, insisting McManus's excessive drinking never affected his work, but Macpherson realised early on that he should learn not just his own lines but McManus's, just in case a speech was suddenly transferred to his character at the last moment.

In 1990 Blythe Duff was introduced as WPC Jackie Reid. The future detective sergeant, and a current mainstay of the series, was a mere uniform copper in 'Death Comes Softly', in which a string of elderly

With his blond hair and sculpted cheekbones, Macpherson was popular with female viewers.

people living alone are murdered. For Blythe, it was an opportunity to try something new after developing her skills in the theatre. Most people she spoke to in the business predicted *Taggart* wouldn't last much longer and she thought she'd be lucky to get a few weeks' work out of it. Her luck's held good for seventeen years.

After Mark McManus died, STV and the ITV network took an unusual gamble: they decided to continue with Reid and Jardine as the joint leads. Many, including the cast themselves, doubted it would work, yet some of the episodes that followed are among the strongest episodes of *Taggart*: cleverly plotted, tense whodunits that keep you guessing to the end.

Over the next few years *Taggart* subtly evolved. No longer a show about a single cop, or a partnership, it was now built around a team. Iain Anders and Robert Robertson stayed, their seniority significant following the loss of McManus, and Jardine and Reid were joined first by Colin McCredie's DC Fraser in 1994 and then by John Michie's DI Robbie Ross in 1998.

Each character brought new qualities to the show. Fraser has an innocent way of always speaking his mind, as well as a wry sense of humour and

DI Robbie Ross introduced a bad-boy element to the team in 1998.

a natty taste in ties. Ross, on the other hand, with his come-to-bed eyes and just-rolled-out-of-bed suits, was the ideal foil for Jardine's by-the-book approach.

'A Scottie dug with a leg at each corner telling you what's what'

In the late 1990s *Taggart* went through a period of major change. Robert Love stepped down from his role as executive producer, and, in 2002, James Macpherson decided to leave after a fifteen-year stint as Jardine. Scottish Media Group (SMG) – the new parent company for STV – realised they needed a fresh approach for a new decade if the programme was to continue to survive in the highly competitive world of commercial television.

A conspiracy of writers, directors and producers decided it was time for Jardine to meet a suitably grisly end. In his place was to be, as the relaunch episode's writer, Stuart Hepburn, puts it, 'a Scottie dug with a leg at each corner telling you what's what'. Alex Norton's Matt Burke is that 'dug', his bark and his bite equally terrifying.

Universally welcomed as a brilliant choice to take on the mantle of the lead detective, Norton's stocky physique and gruff manner left every fan recalling McManus's classic performances. Under his supervision, *Taggart* continues to get high ratings on ITV1 and to be watched all around the world.

Stocky and gruff, Burke's bark really is as bad as his bite.

Chapter 1

Making of a Killer

Our first sight of him is in a cosy living room. A weary, grey-haired man sitting in his dressing gown and slippers, reading a newspaper. His Glaswegian accent is heavy with gravel as he moans about the time his daughter got home the night before. Classical music plays on the stereo – not his choice, you instinctively know, but his wife Jean's. She sits across from him in a wheelchair, pounding industriously at a typewriter on a desk. When the phone rings, the man stands, revealing his slight figure, but on his back is the legend 'Big Daddy' – a tongue-in-cheek reference to the famous wrestler of the day. He turns the music down to nothing, only for Jean to snap at him, telling him to put it back on. Defeated, he complies, but with a sarcastic roll of his eyes to make sure she knows he isn't happy. Then he walks into the hall, picks up the phone and finally introduces himself with just one grunt: 'Taggart.'

A show they can't refuse

When Robert Love joined STV as its head of drama in 1979, it was living in the shadow of its big southern neighbours: Granada, LWT and Thames. Robert was faced with a real challenge: to match them.

'From 1980 I did a series of half-hour plays, *Preview*, that were meant to give a platform to new writers to television – and maybe new directors would get the chance as well,' Robert recalls. 'An actor told me he'd been in an afternoon play in one of the lunchtime theatres in London – a play he'd thought was pretty good – and he thought the writer was a Scot, so I followed up the lead.'

The writer, Glenn Chandler, was still in his twenties and just breaking into theatre and television after giving up his office job at a film company in Piccadilly.

'Robert first discovered me at the Soho Poly Theatre Club in London, where I'd had three one-act plays,' says Glenn. 'None of them was about crime. Robert got in touch and asked me to do some half-hour plays for television. I did three, all quite low-budget, in-the-studio pieces.'

The *Preview* plays were well received, but Robert knew he had to find a bigger concept if he was going to set the heather on fire, north or south of the

border. 'It was a constant struggle to get the network to take our stuff,' he recalls. 'Granada, LWT and Thames didn't want to take things in from Scottish and other regional broadcasters as they had it carved up for themselves. They came up with this system where we had to make the dramas on spec – meaning the company would have to spend the money up front before they would decide whether or not to broadcast it. The best way of operating under that sort of arrangement was to do one-off dramas that became series.

'One was *The House on the Hill* – a different story from a different time period every week. Then, in 1982, we did *Skin Deep*, about two families in Glasgow, and though it had good people in it, it got very badly treated by the network. So I thought, "This is ridiculous: I've got to come up with something they can't refuse."'

It was natural that Robert should consider a detective series as at Thames he'd produced *Van der Valk*, a short-lived but well-liked whodunit set among the canals of Amsterdam.

'I thought, "What is the network short of?" And it didn't have many detective series on the box in those days,' Robert says. 'We were the precursor of *Morse* and Ruth Rendell, remember. And *Frost* was much later, of course. Of the new writers I'd encouraged, Glenn seemed more interested than the others in the forensic side of things, and I decided he'd be worth a go.'

'Robert left the field wide open to me,' says Glenn. 'All he said was it should be about an experienced CID officer and a younger recruit. He told me, "It should have suspense, lead with characters that grip from the first episode and be essentially a whodunit."'

Robert was aware he was asking a lot of this relatively untried writer, but neither man anticipated how tricky developing the right kind of script was going to be. The producer recalls first suggesting a true-crime story. 'There had been a series of murders – in Belgium, I think it was – and the police kept laying traps for the murderer but he always eluded them,' Robert recalls. 'When he did finally get caught, it turned out he was a policeman and that was how he knew how to evade the traps.'

Jim Taggart was the experienced CID officer. Livingstone was his younger recruit.

'Never written a whodunit before'

Working loosely along these lines, Glenn wrote a script for the first hour, and he and Robert agreed things were working well. Halfway into the second hour, however, it fell apart. 'Remember I had never written a whodunit before,' Glenn points out. 'I'd read Agatha Christie and Raymond Chandler, but I'd never attempted to write one.

'Robert realised I was getting into the mire so we had a little pow-wow and we went back to the beginning. I then plotted it out like an architect, so I knew exactly who did it, how it was to finish and where to weave around lots of little subplots. And it worked.'

In *Killer*, a young woman's body is found by a river. Initially, her boyfriend is the prime suspect – he had been out with her the night of her death – but the inquiry is soon widened to include a local ex-con

'I'd read Agatha Christie and Raymond Chandler...'

Clockwise, from above: Glasgow's Maryhill, Springburn, Drumchapel and Milngavie.

with a history of attacking young girls. However, when two further corpses turn up, Jim Taggart realises the guilty party lies elsewhere. Eventually, a well-connected middle-class businessman, Charlie Paterson, played by Roy Hanlon, is revealed as the killer.

'The story grew out of me going round Glasgow,' Glenn explains. 'I was an Edinburgh public schoolboy and didn't know much about the city's raw streets – it is completely different from Edinburgh, even if it is just forty miles away. I spent a week just wandering around Maryhill, Springburn, Drumchapel, Milngavie, which I was convinced was called "Milne-gavvy" in those days [it is pronounced "Mill-guy"], going into pubs and chatting to people.

'A lot of *Killer* came out of those places I visited, writing down elements of stories, going into wee shops and saying, "Oh, yes, those two could be good characters," and letting my imagination go.'

The blueprint for Jim Taggart had been laid down at that first meeting between Robert and Glenn: an older cop who'd worked his way up through the ranks. For Glenn, who'd grown up in Edinburgh and attended a private school, it was natural to make Taggart's sidekick, Detective Sergeant Peter Livingstone, similarly middle class and a university graduate from Edinburgh.

'Plucked from a graveyard in Maryhill'

So where did the name 'Taggart' come from?

'I found all the characters' names in the graveyard in Maryhill. "Jim Taggart" just sounded true to me. The exception was Livingstone, who was named on the train going through to Edinburgh,' Glenn adds with a chuckle.

'The train passed through the town of Livingston and I thought, "That would be good."'

There was a passing thought that English actor Ian Hogg might play the lead detective, but there seems little doubt Mark McManus was always the actor most likely to be offered the role. As Chandler recalls, 'I had to have somebody in mind when I was writing the script and from quite early on the only Scottish actor I could think about was Mark. I'd seen him in a programme, *Strangers*, made by Granada. Don Henderson played the detective in it, and Mark was the chief superintendent.'

'One of the myths about *Taggart* is that other people were offered the role before Mark, but it was only offered to him,' Robert adds. 'It's not that I didn't consider other people; in fact, I was hesitant about Mark at first because height-wise a copper of his generation would have been six feet. Glasgow was one of the last places to reduce the height restriction and they used to say Glasgow cops were all big Highlanders. I also worried that the role might be too close in the public's mind to the one he had in *Strangers*, but in the end they were different enough for that not to matter.'

McManus was sent the script for *Killer*, which he read on a train travelling into London. When he arrived at his destination, he immediately called Robert to say he'd take the part.

D'ye ken?

Scots author William McIlvanney has claimed *Taggart* was derived from his novel *Laidlaw*, and while he's never taken legal action to prove the 'dispute', a Glaswegian urban myth has sprung up to explain it. The suggestion is that the name 'Taggart' was chosen as a specific reference to *Laidlaw*, as both were names of rival car garages in the city at the time.

'I remember first telling Glenn about it,' says Robert Love, 'and he laughed – he's never read *Laidlaw*. At STV, we enquired about rights to it for television, but McIlvanney's agent told us it had been earmarked for a film, which never happened.

'I have read it, but looking back, I don't think it would have stood up as a series. There is a vague similarity, but the character is much more introspective; it was written from a much more intellectualised view of what detective work was like. Also, *Taggart* always had humour. *Laidlaw* didn't have much of that.'

Glenn finds the claim regarding *Laidlaw* baffling: 'I couldn't even drive at the time. I didn't pass my test until a year later. How would I even have known what the city's garages were called?'

Above: Detective Sergeant Peter Livingstone, I presume. With his boss, Jim Taggart. **Opposite:** Jim Taggart, family man, poses with his wife Jean and their daughter.

For an experienced actor, McManus recognised there was plenty in Jim Taggart to get his teeth into. For a start, a man in his prime married to a woman in a wheelchair was an intriguing proposition for an early 1980s audience. It suggested vulnerability and a sense of love and loyalty that contradicted the flinty crag that passed for Taggart's face. However, Chandler's intentions were originally darker than that.

'The character of Jean came out of the plot for the first programme,' the writer explains. 'Young women were being murdered. At the time we didn't know if the series was going to carry on – we thought it might be a one-off – so we thought we'd make Taggart himself a suspect. We decided to give him a wife who is in a wheelchair, so the audience might think, "Yes, he's got problems with his sex life: he might be the killer."'

If the possibility Taggart might be a murderer was sewn in the minds of the audience, it was done so only briefly. For the next eleven years he was to reign supreme as Scotland's premier detective.

D'ye ken?

In eleven years of playing Jim Taggart, Mark McManus never once had the line 'There's been a murrderr.'

Glenn Chandler's Diary

Taggart creator Glenn Chandler kept a diary at the time he was commissioned to write the pilot, *Killer*. In the following extracts he describes the earliest discussions about the show, the development of the script and visiting the set on location in Glasgow.

Friday, 19 March 1982

Met Robert in Covent Garden at five and we went first for tea at a small teashop, then for a drink. We talked at great length about the thriller serial idea, agreeing that it should be a six-part serial with episodes of one-hour duration and that the central characters should be two policemen, one an older, experienced CID officer, the other a younger recruit. Other than that, the field is wide open. Robert says only that it should have suspense, really good characters that grip from the first episode and be essentially a 'whodunit'. What a challenge!

Robert wants it for the network and will attempt to sell the idea to them in April. If this comes off, it will be my biggest writing break ever, so I'm more than conscious that I have to find a real cracker of an idea. None at all as yet, may I add!

Taggart creator Glenn Chandler on set.

Thursday, 4 November 1982

Met Robert Love and Laurence Moody, the director of *Killer*, in London. Had lunch at the Ghurkhas. I liked Laurence — he liked the script of the first episode, with a couple of reservations that I share anyway. He's of the opinion that we need as much film as possible — certainly more than the stingy two days for Episode 2 and three days for Episode 3 that Robert has stipulated. I agree, otherwise we're going to be stuck most of the time in studio sets. In Episode 2, I've kept film to a bare minimum, probably to its detriment. Looks like I'm going to get stuck between them, Robert saying keep film down, and Laurence saying put it in.

Monday, 15 November 1982

Was up at 4.15 a.m., took the train into London and the Underground to Heathrow. Met Laurence Moody in the Shuttle Lounge and we caught the eight fifteen flight to Glasgow.

The Clyde has provided inspiration for some of the grittier *Taggart* moments.

The main part of the day was taken up by driving around Glasgow with Laurence, Gerry Black (she's the production secretary) and Marius (van der Werff), the designer. The purpose was to take Laurence to a lot of the locations I originally visited — we started off with the Kelvin Walkway and the high-rise blocks of flats where Michael and Liz Boyd are supposed to live. I pointed out to Laurence the iron railway bridge from which, in the climax of Episode 3, murderer Charlie Paterson pushes Michael Boyd. Even saw a chap with his dog who could well have been Michael Boyd!

From there we went round Kelvindale, where I pointed out Taggart's house, and then to the Forth and Clyde Canal, the scene of the second murder. Laurence was impressed by the location: the factory in the background, the green and stagnant canal. The body could even be found half in the water.

Took a drive round Bearsden and Milngavie, stamping ground of the murderer Charlie Paterson and his wife, Patricia, and then went on to find a location for the discovery of the third body. Firhill proved disappointing — it was too like the first canal site. Possil Loch was interesting, though, a lonely, marshy place surrounded by low trees and shrubs, with a skyline view of blocks of flats, pylons and rambling cemeteries. It was approachable only by a rough, muddy track, past a farm, the sort of place, I suppose, one might bring a prostitute in a car.

Back to STV and I ran out to get some chicken and chips and pizza for myself, Laurence and Gerry. At the same time I stocked up with tattie scones, haggis and black puddin'!

We are thinking of Ian Hogg for the role of Taggart — alas, he isn't a Scot. Robert's arranged for him to telephone from London and put on a Glasgow accent!

Friday, 3 December 1982

In the afternoon I took the bike into London to meet Robert and Laurence at Old Burlington Street. Had a meeting about the script, which was useful, and made a lot of all the amendments necessary — Laurence read out the casting. I'm over the moon about Mick McManus [sic] as Taggart. He's very keen apparently, and was surprised to be offered the part, since he and Laurence Moody had an argument on the last thing they worked on.

Wednesday, 5 January 1983

The day of the *Killer* read-through in Glasgow, at STV. It's the biggest cast that's ever been assembled for anything I've written. I felt quite awestruck.

Hearing it read cold, episode by episode, didn't give me a very real impression of how it might eventually sound or look. But Mark McManus congratulated me on a 'cracking story', and I received other compliments — no one, it seemed, had guessed the identity of the murderer. Many had plumbed for Taggart himself, and a few thought it was Patricia Paterson. A relief, I thought. However, having heard it read, I'm of the opinion — and both Robert and Laurence agree — that Episode 2 in particular needs some trimming of words, and the whole denouement needs restructuring to make it clearer to the audience.

Laurence asked wisely that, unlike the majority of our national secrets, the identity of the murderer be kept secret by everyone involved!

Thursday, 6 January 1983

My first day out with a film unit, and a rigorous experience! Laurence called at the flat just after eight, and the three of us walked down to a scrap yard where the unit were gathering to film the minor but important sequence where the bag of the second murder victim, containing vital evidence, turns up among some rubbish. It entailed Joe Miller, the unit production manager, climbing up into the jaws of a crane and inserting the bag in a mass of scrap metal.

The weather was kind to us for a while, but soon we were lashed by a cold wind and snow. The snow continued in heavy flurries for the rest of the day at the main location, Muirpark Street, the site of McGowan's shop. A small, derelict, unoccupied general store had been dressed perfectly to look like one of those backstreet shops that depend solely on the goodwill of the community for its survival.

I must say, it was exciting for me, even if it was routine stuff for everyone else. There was a lot of standing about waiting for things to happen, but it was fun being part of it all, seeing it all start — and being in the centre of Maryhill, with shoppers, kids and other passers-by stopping to gawk and ask questions; it was like being God come down among the natives.

I thought that Frank Wylie made a perfect McGowan — frighteningly pathetic. And Mark McManus and Neil (Alastair) Duncan made a well-matched Taggart and Livingstone.

Fun moments of the day: a scene where Mark McManus had to get into his car, leaving Neil Duncan standing in the road, and deliver the line 'You want to get to know Glasgow? Walk,' before driving off. Would the car get into gear? I think we did about ten takes before the car was finally pulled off by a knotted rope heaved by eight people.

Livingstone and Taggart made a well-matched team.

Tuesday, 1 February 1983

The second day in the studio, and the end of the Boyds' flat scenes. I wonder how convincingly we'll establish in viewers' minds that Michael Boyd is the killer. We also recorded the small scene in the mortuary, where the Ballantynes, played by Hugh Martin and Mary MacLeod, identify their dead daughter. The victim appears on a television screen, which strikes me as being a horribly impersonal way of identifying a dead loved one. I think I'd sooner see the drawer come out and the sheet drawn back, as it usually happens in the 'movies'.

In the afternoon, I went up with Anne Fielding, the casting director, to the film editing room and saw all the rushes. I was most impressed! Laurence has certainly underplayed everything very nicely — particularly the relationship between Taggart and Livingstone — and the mood of a bleak, wintry Glasgow is nicely caught in the locations. The murder victims looked very dead! And quite grisly, too.

Friday, 4 February 1983

The morning was spent at a tower block by the river Kelvin, filming the Boyd scenes. What an ice-cold wind! We were all freezing. Gerard Kelly was almost hysterical. Luckily the coach was warm, so

The grisly element of *Taggart* has kept fans hooked for twenty-five years.

at lunchtime we were able to sit and watch a video of An American Werewolf in London.

As darkness fell, the film unit moved down to the banks of the Kelvin for the fight in the river and the arrival of the police en masse. It was an exciting occasion. Both Mark McManus and Roy Hanlon had doubles to perform the stunts, like falling into the river from an eight-foot-high bank, and there was a stunt arranger on hand to mastermind things. Crowds of kids gathered on the bridges above. The excitement of the occasion was marred by the electricians' decision to pull the plug at ten o'clock on the dot. If we'd been able to film until midnight, we could have got the whole sequence completed. I asked Robert why they weren't prepared to work overtime for what would have amounted to double time — he said they were paid so much it didn't make any difference. Besides, they were cold and wet. Ah, what a shame. So was everyone.

Tuesday, 1 March 1983

I flew to Glasgow this morning for the final stages of *Killer* recording. Today we recorded the scenes in the video shop. Unhappy to learn that Bute, Joe Miller's dog, and the canine star of *Killer* has disappeared from home — with one final scene yet to do. Gerard Kelly had to walk into the video shop with a fluffy toy on the end of a lead to give the impression Bute was there (though unseen on camera) and couldn't say his lines for feeling ridiculous.

Thursday, 3 March 1983

The final day. The key scene of *Killer* went beautifully — this was the scene where Patricia

Paterson discovers the cigarette lighter belonging to her dead lover in Charlie's desk. There was one final take that we all felt instinctively could not be bettered. Rolled a few credits, went up to the film viewing room with Laurence to see the dubbed beating-up scene (lots of crunchy splats and punches), and then that was it. An anticlimax, in a way. I killed a couple of hours in the office working on *Angels*, then went over to Carruthers with Laurence. I think he's done a smashing job of directing *Killer* — we haven't really had any disagreements. Only the odd difference of opinion on minor points. Robert's secretary, Margaret, came over too, and we got fairly pissed even before the meal.

Robert had given me the option of going back to his flat to freshen up first, but nothing quite takes the heat out of a good evening than freshening up before it! Laurence, Margaret and I took a taxi to the Ubiquitous Chip (a restaurant in Glasgow's West End), joined the others — Mark McManus, Neil Duncan, Tom Watson, Anne Kidd and Gerard Kelly were there. The meal was fair, nothing startling, but then through the alcoholic haze I didn't really bother that much. It was the event that mattered. The end of recording *Killer*. A sad event — but full of optimism. Jimmy Stewart, the cameraman, told me tonight that what I had written was a good old-fashioned murder mystery — of the kind rarely seen on television nowadays. Laurence sees no reason whatsoever why the characters of Taggart, Livingstone and Murray shouldn't run into a series — Scotland desperately needs a thriller-police series of its own. If STV can't handle it, then Laurence feels an independent film company might. All early days, though.

Saying goodbye was sad. Mark McManus became a bit emotional — he said that an actor's life was all about 'endings' — finishing this and finishing that. I told him that for every ending there was always a new beginning. Robert chipped in with the statement that the guy who works in the same office all his life enjoys no new beginnings, doesn't have the opportunity to begin new ventures, as actors, writers, producers and directors do. We ought to consider ourselves fortunate.

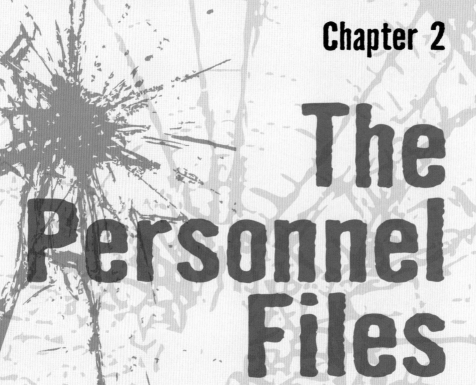

Chapter 2

The Personnel Files

The current incumbent of the *Taggart* mortuary is
Dr Magnus Baird, a man cut of the same cloth as
Dr Stephen Andrews. Professional, cool-headed
and direct, he's as sharp as they come.

Actor Michael MacKenzie joined the
cast for the sexual intrigue of 'The
Ties That Bind' (2005), but it wasn't
his first time on the show. He'd
appeared twice before in minor
roles in 'Death Benefits' (1993) and
'The Killing Philosophy' (1987).

Michael has been a regular on
television since the early 1970s,
with roles in shows like *Cardiac
Arrest* and *Hamish Macbeth*. Viewers of a

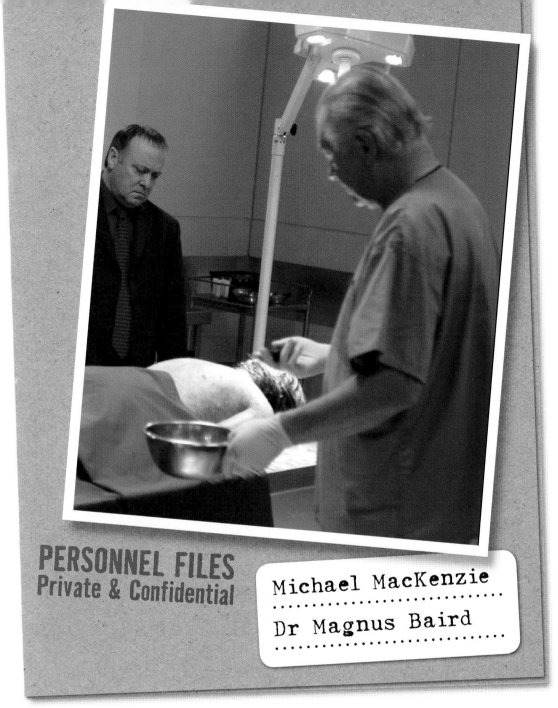

Michael MacKenzie
·····························
Dr Magnus Baird
·····························

certain age might remember him, however, from a long-running ITV children's series *Ace of Wands* (1970–2), in which he played the lead role of Tarot, a magician who battled master criminals. The comic-book gothic style of the series won a big teatime following – the show rivalled *Dr Who* – but it was ultimately replaced by *Tomorrow's People*.

Dr Baird shows DCI Burke the autopsy ropes.

Alex Norton
....
DCI Matt Burke
....

Alex Norton's family came from a tough district of the South Side of Glasgow. While he was at school, Alex's father, a plumber, advised him to get a trade and was shocked when Alex revealed he wanted to be an actor. It wasn't until Alex landed a role in a popular television series that his straight-talking dad began to accept his son might be a success in his chosen profession after all. That show was *Taggart*, and Alex was playing a dodgy butcher with a corpse in his doocot.

Alex was born in 1950 in the Gorbals, the elder of two boys, his family moving to nearby Pollokshaws not long after.

He was thirteen when he first started going to a youth drama club; his mum, Sadie, encouraged his ambitions to go on and be an actor. Tragically, she died when Alex was just fifteen, and he lost his champion. His father disapproved of the idea, insisting the youngster should get a trade. It left father and son at loggerheads.

'There were no theatrical connections in my family, but I knew there was no option for me: the bug took. My dad thought if you wanted to be an actor you had to be a "poof". He had been a plumber, then he'd had trouble with his back and so he worked as a general labourer in factories. That's what he did most of his working life. He always told me to get a trade, because that was the done thing then.

'It was a big deal for me to be in *Taggart* in 1985 [his first episode, "Knife Edge", was broadcast in 1986], a real breakthrough; it convinced my dad it was OK for me to be an actor because his mates had told him they'd seen me in it and that I was good.'

Looking back now, Alex can see his father had his best interests at heart. 'He thought becoming an actor was totally unrealistic, and I still think it is unrealistic,' he comments. 'If anyone tells me they are thinking about becoming an actor, I tell them that if there is anything else they think they might want to do instead, and be happy, then for God's sake do it. But you know, it's a vocation, and if you feel there's nothing else that will give you the satisfaction, then fine.'

Alex landed his first TV job at the age of fourteen in STV's popular *Dr Finlay's Casebook*. Not long after, he knocked on the door of Glasgow's Pavilion Theatre and asked for a job. They gave him one sweeping the stage. Far from daunted, he used the opportunity to learn the mysteries of stagecraft as he went along.

A little later he ran into Billy Connolly on the folk-music circuit. Alex could already play the guitar, and Billy showed him how to play the banjo.

He didn't want to stick around his home city long, however, opting instead to move to London, where there was more chance of work. He was eighteen years old, owned a second-hand taxi, which he filled with his belongings, and he was off.

'The Glasgow I left in the 1960s was this dark, sombre place. Though probably no more violent than it is now, the violence was one reason why I wanted to move to London – there was one time I thought I was going to get chopped up,' he recalls.

Alex had been out for a night with a pal, the actor Brian Pettifer. The lads had dressed up to impress, having bought themselves brightly coloured military jackets in the style of the Beatles' Sergeant Pepper.

> 'The Glasgow I left in the 1960s was this dark, sombre place.'

'I tell you, it took a lot of bottle to walk through Glasgow like that in 1967,' Alex laughs. 'These guys stopped us and said, "Nice jackets, boys, but I'm afraid they were stolen from us at a party last night." I told them, "Where's your proof?" and this one guy brought back his coat to show us he had a sword underneath. We saw a policeman and just ran towards him, shouting, "They're going to kill us." The policeman looked us up and down and said, "In those jackets? What do you expect?"'

'In the 1960s the first thing you did if you wanted to be an actor was lose the regional accent.'

In the 1970s Alex gained an excellent reputation in the theatre as a writer as well as an actor. Along with his close pal, and *Sea of Souls* star, Bill Paterson, he was among the founders of the 7:84 Theatre Company, a politically motivated group that launched with John McGrath's 1973 play *The Cheviot, The Stag and the Black, Black Oil*. Alex won praise for his own writing, too, when he adapted the book *No Mean City*, which was revived at Glasgow's Citizens' Theatre as recently as 2006. He went on to write for STV's kids' series *Dramarama* in the 1980s.

He teamed up again with Connolly, starring together in the live extravaganza that was *The Welly Boot Show*; they were reunited again on television in 1993's *Down Among the Big Boys*. The 1970s also brought plenty of film and television work, including *The Sweeney*, *Play for Today* and a bit-part in *The Virgin Soldiers* alongside another unknown extra, David Bowie.

Ten years after leaving home, he was appearing in John Byrne's play *Writer's Cramp* when his father joined the audience. They went out for a drink afterwards and his father told him, 'See all that trouble we had when you were young? Well, I'm glad to say I was wrong.' The reconciliation, Alex says, brought tears to his eyes.

In the 1980s Alex's profile was raised thanks to the likes of *Taggart*, Bill Forsyth's landmark comedy *Gregory's Girl* and the first series of Rowan Atkinson's *The Black Adder*, in which he played a terrible Scot, the fearsome McAngus.

Alex credits *Taggart* – and the likes of Sean Connery – for helping to 'nail that bloody terrible, hoary myth' that people in England couldn't understand a Scottish accent.

'In the 1960s the first thing you did if you wanted to be an actor was lose the regional accent, but because of people like Connery and McManus, people like me started thinking the accent was maybe an advantage rather than a disadvantage.'

In the 1990s his acting – complete with Glaswegian accent – took over from other talents and he won roles in Hollywood movies, including *Patriot Games* with Harrison Ford, *White Hunter Black Heart* with Clint Eastwood and *Braveheart* with Mel Gibson, as well as *Beautiful Creatures* and *The Scarlet Pimpernel*.

He joined *Taggart* as DCI Burke in 2001, but has still found the time to appear as Napoleon in *The Count of Monte Cristo* (2002) and as a doomed seafarer in *Pirates of the Caribbean: Dead Man's Chest* (2006).

Alex first met his wife, Sally Kinghorn, while working on a play at the end of the 1970s. He'd fancied her and asked her out, but the fact he already had a girlfriend proved a stumbling block. They met again on the set of *Strangers* three years later, in 1981 – the ITV drama that happened to star Mark McManus – and he fell for her again. This time he launched a serious, long-term campaign to woo her, with the result they are now married and have three children.

Taggart has meant a degree of upheaval for the Norton family. But as his sons – Jock, fifteen, Rory, thirteen, and Jamie, eight – are rooted in London, he decided from the beginning to commute rather than move. Filming means flying to Glasgow early on the Monday, then returning last thing on Friday. 'But the weekends at home are a great compensation,' he says.

Burke interrogates an unfortunate suspect in 'Users and Losers'.

Tamara Kennedy
....
Sheila Crombie
....

DCI Matt Burke arrived at the offices of Glasgow CID with a face of granite. Who knew there was a human being underneath? Well, Sheila Crombie did. At least, that's the way it appeared when the forensics expert first made her appearance in 2002. 'Now don't rush to conclusions, Matthew,' she tells Burke, an exchange that lets Reid, Ross and Fraser know all they need to know. This was a woman who had a history with Burke from his Special Branch days...How intriguing.

Tamara Kennedy had appeared in *Taggart* before, in 1999, playing Dr Fellowes in the mystery 'Fearful Lightning'. Her return as Sheila, however, marked a shift for the programme. It was the first time a regular character had taken the role once performed by Dr Stephen Andrews following Robert Robertson's death in 2001 – that of the quiet voice of scientific authority. Reflecting the times, Sheila was a) a woman, b) not worried about expressing her opinion and c) not a pathologist at all, but a forensic specialist. Since the late 1990s forensics had become increasingly important to detective work, and *Taggart* needed to reflect that.

Edinburgh-born Tamara, who was previously known to Scottish audiences as Joanna Ross-Gifford in *Take the High Road* and as a successful voiceover specialist, was extremely popular with fans, many of whom wanted to know more about Sheila's 'relationship' with Burke.

But before anything could come of the flirtation, it was decided Sheila would move on and Tamara left the cast.

Sheila: 'Go away. I'm busy.'
Burke: 'Even for me?'
Sheila: 'You're not the only copper with a murder case round here, you know.'
Burke: 'But the thing is, what I really need to know is...what's that perfume you're wearing?'

'Fade to Black' (2002)

When Mark McManus died, there was some speculation down at the bookies on Maryhill Road as to who would replace him. A few quid was wasted on Sean Connery – something of an outsider, his salary a bit steep for STV – but Maurice Roëves and Bill Paterson were the names punters took seriously. One not considered was that of Colin McCredie, but it was the young unknown from Perth who had the job of stepping into McManus's shoes.

As Fraser, Colin McCredie is the perpetual wee brother of the *Taggart* family. Born in 1972 in Perth, the youngest of five children, it's a role he was already used to. His mum, Bridie, died when he was just eleven, leaving his father, Norman, to raise the kids on his own.

'It was pretty hard for my dad, having to bring up me and my brothers and sisters, and he'd nursed my mother, who'd had cancer, for a couple of years. But one good thing about coming from a big family is that you get a

PERSONNEL FILES
Private & Confidential

Colin McCredie
....
DC Fraser
....

McCredie's Fraser assumes the position alongside Burke and Reid.

lot of support. As a wee boy, losing your mum creates a big hole in your life,' Colin observes, 'but at the time I just wouldn't mention her death. I thought if I didn't talk about it, I wouldn't get upset, but it's not a good way of dealing with it.'

Colin was able to find distraction in a new passion: acting. His sister Anne worked as an usherette and later as stage manager at the Perth Theatre. 'She used to get tickets for me for matinées,' he recalls. 'I used to go and get lost in another world. Back then they did Agatha Christie and George Bernard Shaw – with proper sets and the proscenium arch. I guess now it would seem old-fashioned, but at the time I thought it was great.'

From the age of twelve he supplemented this interest by attending the Scottish Youth Theatre drama workshops, leading to roles as a child actor. He recalls a scene at Glasgow's Kelvinbridge Art Gallery and Museum with *Crime and Retribution*-star David Hayman for the BBC's *Holy City* and a spot in panto alongside the late Rikki Fulton.

Through acting he met Ewan McGregor – another local boy. 'Ewan left school after fourth year to work at the Perth Theatre,' Colin recalls. 'I guess he'd be sixteen and I was fifteen at the time. He went to a foundation course at Kirkcaldy and then on to London. I still keep in touch, though I guess I see his mum more than him these days!'

Colin won a place at Glasgow's RSAMD, where he claims he worked hard without ever being 'one of the favourites'. After graduation, however, he found he had the knack of getting jobs. There was a brief role in the film *Shallow Grave*, in which he got to punch his old mate McGregor. 'Darth Maul couldn't beat him, but I could,' Colin laughs. And a part in the film *Small Faces*, directed by Gillies MacKinnon, alongside Kevin McKidd and Laura Fraser.

For his break in *Taggart*, he credits his acting mate Tony Curran. 'Tony's based over in Hollywood, now making films like *Miami Vice*,' Colin says. 'But just after finishing college he and I went up for the same small role in *Dr Finlay's Casebook*. Tony got the part ahead of me, but then told them

'I grew up with *Taggart*. I was eleven when it first appeared and it's been part of my life since then.'

he was also in a play and had to finish at six p.m. They said, "No way," and called me instead. Robert Love saw me in that part and got me in to do *Taggart* afterwards.'

Colin did two brief cameos in *Taggart* – most notably in 'Hellfire' (1994) – before being cast as DC Fraser.

'I grew up with *Taggart*. I was eleven when it first appeared and it's been part of my life since then,' he recalls. 'When I was at school and at drama school, *Taggart* was something I always watched. And I always hoped I'd be in it.'

The good news he'd landed a bigger part as a policeman, however, was tempered by the death of Mark McManus. 'I'd seen Mark at the read-throughs and knew he wasn't very well. When he died, it was naturally upsetting for everyone who'd worked with him, but for me, I just assumed I'd had the worst kind of luck – that I'd got this great part, only for the series to end.' But as DC Fraser, McCredie helped the drama go from strength to strength.

Initially, the young detective was played far more obviously for laughs than he is now. 'That was how I was being directed,' Colin points out. '*Taggart* has always had that black humour.' But 1996's 'Angel Eyes' brought an unexpected twist that gave Fraser instant depth: during the hunt for a gay serial killer, he was forced to come out of the closet himself.

Although unprepared for this development at the time, Colin took it in his stride and believes the audience did, too. Indeed, he reckons many *Taggart* viewers probably forget Fraser's sexual preference as it is seldom referred to and hardly ever a feature of a plot. It wasn't until 2005, for instance – nearly ten years after

D'ye ken?

When Colin joined *Taggart*, he had only been out of drama school for eighteen months. He is now the second-longest-serving cast member with twelve years on the show, giving him a financial security many actors can only dream of. '*Taggart* does tend to mean you are limited in what other things you can do,' he says, 'but I enjoy it, it suits me, and it is a great show.'

coming out – that he finally kissed his first man on screen, when, in the episode 'A Taste of Money', an old boyfriend discovers the body of a murdered restaurant critic.

This was an event of some amusement to his wife, Simone, whom he married in 2002 and with whom he has a two-year-old daughter, Maisie. Simone surprised Colin by declaring she was uncomfortable with the idea of him kissing the actor Paul Ireland. 'But why?' he wanted to know. 'Because I fancy him myself,' she told him.

Away from the small screen, Colin takes theatre roles when he can and enjoys a family life in the West End of Glasgow, a short drive from where *Taggart* is filmed. He is a keen music fan, particularly of the city's indie bands, and was once surprised to be spotted by Texas singer Sharleen Spiteri. 'She told me she was a fan of *Taggart*!'

When James Macpherson left grammar school in his native Hamilton, his parents told him to get a trade, so at the age of seventeen he worked briefly at an engineering company, before landing a job at Glasgow's Southern General Hospital. He was based in the Neuropathology department, where he attended post-mortems. He never guessed that one day he'd be back in mortuaries filming scenes for Britain's best-loved television detective series.

James Macpherson stayed in the lab for five years – regularly sitting exams and keeping the textbooks as bedside reading because he loved the science so much. It was in this period that he met Jacqueline, who was to become his wife and the mother of his three children, Jamie, Kate and Jack.

PERSONNEL FILES
Private & Confidential

James Macpherson

DCI Mike Jardine

James's future took a twist his parents didn't quite expect when he decided to try out for a place at the Royal Scottish Academy of Music and Drama – his performance experience at that time limited to choirs and am dram. He'd stopped looking through microscopes for a living; soon he was about to start living under one.

He did well in a class that included John Hannah, winning a move to London to work with the BBC's radio drama department, where he got a regular role in the Radio 4 soap *Citizens*. However, Robert Love had seen him at college and invited him to audition for one of STV's children's productions, *Dramarama*, auditioning for director Haldane Duncan.

He didn't get the part and moved back to Scotland, only for the work to dry up altogether. He took a job at a friend's engineering company to tide himself over, and had more or less decided on a life without acting when STV called him back in. 'Haldane Duncan was directing the next *Taggart* and wanted to see me again,' he recalls. 'This was for the role of a young DS. I wasn't so much the replacement for Peter Livingstone at the time as a replacement for Stuart Hepburn's DS Kenny Forfar.' James was twenty-six when he was cast as Jardine.

His first *Taggart* was 'The Killing Philosophy' (1987), a dark tale featuring the mysterious 'Glasgow Bowman', who terrorises Glasgow's leafy suburb of Bearsden armed with a hand-held crossbow. Typically, it was shot in the middle of the Scottish winter in an almost permanent freezing drizzle.

'It was guerrilla tactics. When we were out filming, we'd just be out in the street, and between takes Mark and I would go and sit in the car to keep warm. There were no toilets or Winnebagos or anything like that: we went out and did the shot and came back.

'There was one day we were filming a scene under the arches at Kelvinbridge and there was a blackened body that had been burned and Jardine had to faint. Well, I had gastroenteritis that day, so no acting was required. Joe Miller, *Taggart*'s legendary location manager, took me into the Doublet pub and announced to everyone in the bar, "Can we use your toilet? The boy's got diarrhoea!"'

James was surprised to find his science background of benefit to the show. Back then they used real mortuaries for scenes with Dr Stephen Andrews, played by Robert Robertson, gazing at corpses. But no one was keen to walk into one without checking the real-life bodies had been put away first.

'I remember the crew used to send me in to check the room was empty before they went through to set up,' he laughs. 'They thought as I'd done it before that I could handle it. One time a pathologist was still working on something. I explained to him we were going to film a scene with a

'Out filming, we'd just be out in the street, and between takes Mark and I would go and sit in the car to keep warm.'

Macpherson and McManus got on famously.

mummified baby, one that had been found in an attic. As it happens, that's exactly what the pathologist had been looking at when we arrived, a real case of it. Apparently, they were common – the result of desperate teenage mums saying to themselves, "What am I going to do?"'

James quickly grew into the role of Jardine – helped by the fact he got on famously with his co-star, McManus, godfather to James's daughter, Kate, and spending regular weekends at the elder actor's country cottage.

James admits that the impact *Taggart* was to have on all aspects of his life came as a bit of a shock. A naturally very private person, living in Glasgow gradually turned into something of a goldfish bowl. 'When I started, there was no such thing as celebrity. In 1986 you got your picture in the *Daily Record* and that was it. It was the work that was the most important thing – not the fact you were out in a nightclub.'

However, as the years went by and *Taggart* grew in popularity, James found he couldn't ignore the celebrity issue. 'I've often said I wouldn't be an actor on *Taggart* again because the attention you get is too much. I had no idea what anonymity was and how precious it was until I lost it. I found I'd be out with my kids and people were shouting at me in the street, and that was a pain. I never got any bad chat, but I used to go to Cape Cod on my holidays because there I could be me without anyone knowing who I was – without worrying about anyone looking at me.'

There were other aspects of fame he found puzzling. He remembers attending a charity night with Mark McManus, and afterwards going outside to head home. 'People had kept buying me lagers and I'd had too much to drink,' says James. 'Mark sees me outside and says to me, "What you doing?" I said, "Waiting for a bus." Mark just looks at me and says, "You're the star of *Taggart*: you're getting a taxi."'

Later in his career, he recalls being surprised on his doorstep by Keith Chegwin. 'It was breakfast, the kids were getting ready for school, it was the usual chaos, and I think I was holding Jack in my arms. And then the doorbell goes and it's Cheggers from *The Big Breakfast* outside doing some "we're surprising a famous person at home" item.'

To his credit, James took the invasion of his privacy with good humour, happily agreeing to try his hand at being a cowboy. 'They'd built a full rodeo in my next-door neighbour's garden,' he explains. 'I think I'd maybe said something in the past about liking westerns – well, I had to get up and ride this horse. It was reasonably funny.

'One of my regrets is that I never took up their offer of hosting the show for a week – they seemed to think I'd been a good sport. But I'd thought, "Present *The Big Breakfast*? No way, I'm an actor! I wouldn't be so bothered by that now.'

After quitting the show in 2001, James admits he has tended to keep the programme at a distance. 'I had fifteen years on *Taggart* and I guess eleven were great, and that's pretty good for any job. It allowed me to be reasonably affluent at a time when my kids were growing up – and I'm very proud of the product. My big problem with *Taggart* is that if it comes on and I'm not prepared for it, I'll see Mark on screen and it makes me want to cry. There are hundreds of emotions. I wish I'd had more time with him. It's like your father dying. You think, "I should have done things differently."'

James is now a fellow at his old drama college, the RSAMD, and appears regularly on stage, radio and television. Recently he has taken up the role of another Scottish detective – as the voice of Ian Rankin's Rebus on audiobook.

He regularly appears on stage in Scotland and presents documentaries and programmes for television and radio. In his spare time he remains a keen scientist. He's also part of Glasgow's most exclusive pub rock band, MLC. 'It stands for "Mid-Life Crisis", for obvious reasons,' James laughs.

It features former Scotland rugby player and radio broadcaster Johnnie Beattie, Tommy Cunningham, formerly of Wet Wet Wet, and BBC Scotland newsreader Jackie Byrd. They first got together at a school gala concert and they now play several times a year at events across Glasgow.

'If it was up to Johnnie, we'd be out there every week,' James laughs. 'But as you can tell from our name, it's not exactly a career!'

'When I started, there was no such thing as celebrity. In 1986 you got your picture in the *Daily Record* and that was it.'

Macpherson in 'Fearful Lightning', 1999.

PERSONNEL FILES
Private & Confidential

Lesley Harcourt
....
Gemma Kerr
....

Beautiful, young and brilliant, Gemma Kerr is *Taggart*'s forensic scientist with attitude. Introduced in the 2004 episode 'Saints and Sinners', Gemma is the kind of woman Robbie Ross dreams about. And that's all he's going to have the chance to do, because while Gemma Kerr might not be opposed to the odd bit of flirting, it's forensics she's really interested in.

Lesley Harcourt was born in Glasgow but moved with her family to Harrogate when she was eight, returning to Scotland to study drama in Edinburgh when she was eighteen.

She'd already relocated to London to pursue acting work by the time she was offered the role of Gemma, but considering she had been working as a waitress for fifteen months by that time, she was only too happy to commute between the cities during filming.

'Saints and Sinners' was her second *Taggart* role. Only just over a year before, in 'An Eye for an Eye', she played Dr Roberta Paton, a partner at a women's health clinic who is shot when she walks into a booby-trapped room, then murdered while still recovering in hospital by being pushed down the stairs while strapped to a wheelchair.

Such a bloody way to go should have prepared the actress for what was to come when she accepted the role of Gemma, the woman destined to be first on the scene at every subsequent murder for twelve episodes. However, the graphic nature of *Taggart* was still a shock – partly because when she was growing up, her parents never let her watch the programme as it was too grisly. 'Knowing what I know now, and from what I've seen on set, they were right to not let me watch it, because it's pretty horrible!' she commented. 'When you walk into a room where someone has been brutally murdered…Well, thank goodness for fake blood. I don't think I could cope if I saw anything like that in real life. Sometimes I catch myself among all these dead bodies and wonder, "What *are* we all doing for a living?"'

Gemma was a popular addition to the team. Robbie Ross couldn't take his eyes off her, though the scriptwriters always made sure she kept him at bay. And even Matt Burke showed her a great deal of respect, turning to her to make sense of evidence or to accompany him to the scene of a crime.

However, there's a natural limit to what a forensic scientist can do with *Taggart*. 'I wanted to do high drama, cry, scream, the lot, and not just swat off the attentions of Robbie Ross for ever more. But the show taught me so much and raised my profile beyond belief,' she says.

Lesley left the show for a stint on BBC soap *Doctors* and to join a touring stage production of *Cat on a Hot Tin Roof*, taking the Elizabeth Taylor lead role.

If Robbie had known, you could bet he'd have bought tickets.

'Thank goodness for fake blood. I don't think I could cope if I saw anything like that in real life.'

It wasn't just murders Jim Taggart had to put up with; in the beginning he also had to suffer the great-long-drink-of-water Edinburgh University student who'd been assigned to work with him, Detective Sergeant Peter Livingstone: the first sidekick.

Livingstone was everything Taggart was not. He was young, tall, good-looking, privileged – a 'flier' on the fast track to promotion. But worst of all

Alastair Duncan
. . . .
DS Peter Livingstone
. . . .

he was inexperienced and had the temerity to get on with Jim's family. Jean and Livingstone talked about *art* together. And his daughter? Jim didn't dare think what *they* talked about.

Alastair now lives in Hollywood. But why the name change?

'I was always Alastair, but Equity wouldn't allow me to use the name because someone else had it,' he explains. 'When I came over to America, I traced the actor and it turned out he was an Australian who wasn't working any more. I eventually got my name back, though if you look on the Internet Movie Database, you'll see I've still got some of his credits and not all of mine. It makes it look like a very odd career indeed. But I had realised I didn't like being Neil; it wasn't my name.'

He was just twenty-five when STV's head of drama, Robert Love, and director Laurence Moody recruited him for *Killer*. Like the character he played, he admits to being a bit green. 'Oh, I had no idea what I was doing: I was flying blind,' he recalls. 'Fortunately, I had Mark guiding me.'

Livingstone's prickly relationship with the elder detective proved to be one of the programme's highlights in the early years. You tuned in wondering if wee Jim was going to stick one on big Pete's nose.

'It's a story that has been told so many times,' Alastair points out. '*The Streets of San Francisco*, for instance, and I later did a film with Rutger Hauer that was the exact same deal. It's a great, classic, conflicted relationship. You have the older man who knows it all but who can't express it, and the younger one, the neophyte, who thinks he knows it all and who talks all the time but who actually knows nothing and has to be taught.'

Filming on location in those early days was quite an eye-opener for the young actor. 'We had nothing,' he says. 'We basically went and sat in a car to keep warm. I don't think I ever had a Winnebago, ever. Between scenes we'd go sit in the pub, or just sit where we could.

'When we were doing *Killer*, Mark had to jump into the river Kelvin to trap the murderer at the very end. It was freezing, as it always was, and we were shooting at midnight, but there were kids hanging off the footbridge in their T-shirts. I had layers on with thermal vests and I remember thinking, "They are insane."'

Despite *Taggart's* success with audiences, in 1986 Alastair decided to leave the show, making his last appearance in 'The Killing Philosophy', broadcast in April 1987. His co-star took him aside and tried to talk him out of it, but the young actor's mind was made up.

'I recognised it was going to be exactly what it was – I wasn't going to be allowed to spread my wings and change. There was a certain element of it that was formulaic and I couldn't go outside those parameters,' he explains. 'I wanted to do something different and I didn't want to get typecast. It was a difficult decision, but I had no doubts it was the right one. Actually, it was

Another day, another corpse for Alastair Duncan's Livingstone.

a no-brainer for me. Whenever I've made those decisions – to leave *Taggart*, to come to America – I've never had any angst with it.'

Considering *Taggart*'s longevity – and the way Blythe Duff and James Macpherson assumed the lead following Mark McManus's death – had he stuck with the programme, Livingstone might have eventually found himself as a DCI.

'I tell you what, when I look back in fifty years and think of the amount of money I might have earned in *Taggart*, I might say, "Oh, damn,"' Alastair laughs. 'But I wouldn't have the wife I have and the life I have now if I'd stayed. There are things about it I regret, but I don't regret leaving.'

After *Taggart*, Alastair first relocated to London and then to Hollywood, where he has enjoyed a successful career in television and stage.

While working on a play in Los Angeles, he met and fell in love with the *Deadwood* actress Anna Gunn. They married and now have two children, Emma Grace and Isla Rose.

'I now have a house right under the Hollywood sign,' says Alastair. 'My wife being an actress has never been a problem; I'm not competitive that way – I never felt jealous if she got a wonderful job. But now there's none of that anyway.'

Alastair returned to the Livingstone role once after meeting producer Robert Love on a flying visit to Glasgow – incredibly, they bumped into each other in a supermarket. In 'Forbidden Fruit' (1994), set around a fertility clinic, Taggart's former sidekick had left the police to become a freelance security expert with a low sperm count. 'When I read that bit, I thought, "No!" But then decided what the hell!'

It was to be his last appearance, not just in *Taggart* but in a major British production. Despite working steadily for most of the past twenty years as an actor, and collecting various awards, Alastair has limited his performances in the past two years to voiceovers on cartoons and computer games. His full-time job is no longer acting, but as a realtor in the tough Los Angeles property market, and he's loving every minute of it.

For 'Knife Edge' (1986), Alastair had to be kissed full on the mouth by a hairy Hell's Angel.

'I got bored with acting,' he explains. 'I was offered a really nice series, and I thought, "No, I don't want to do it." And if I didn't want to do a good series, why was I in it at all? The great thing about what I do now is that I can create my own schedule, and to an extent as an actor you create your own schedule, so Anna and I get a lot more time to see each other.'

Alastair's parents, Ann and Archie, a retired professor of Scottish history, still live in Glasgow, and he remains good friends with Stirling-based Stuart Hepburn, who as DS Kenny Forfar was his co-star in the early episodes of *Taggart* and a regular writer for the series. But with a sister in Spain and a brother in Australia, he admits trips home to Scotland are few and far between.

'I don't miss Glasgow as such,' he says, 'but I miss people, and going to the pub. I miss London for the same reason. Whenever I go back I love it, but after a couple of weeks I miss being at home. This is my home now.'

Iain Anders
....
Superintendent McVitie
....

From 1985 to his untimely death in 1997 Iain Anders played Superintendent McVitie, 'the Biscuit', and provided the ultimate voice of authority in *Taggart*. He was the man to keep Jim Taggart in check and to corral the youngsters, Jardine and Reid, when they took over following Jim Taggart's death in 1994.

Born Iain Anders Robertson, of Scottish background, in London in 1933, he was an expert bridge player and even used to teach the game. He lived in Chichester and worked in London while not filming *Taggart* in Glasgow. Only a part-time actor, Iain's day job was as a legal managing clerk, which led him to spending a lot of time in police stations stopping suspected criminals speaking to policemen. 'Most of my clients think it's a great laugh I play a copper on television,' he once said. He played a policeman in several other shows, too, including *Z Cars*, *Softly Softly*, *Juliet Bravo* and *Shoestring*.

From his first appearance – he replaced Tom Watson (Superintendent Murray, 'the Mint') in the second *Taggart* three-parter (or the third if you include *Killer*), 'Murder in Season', with Isla Blair and Ken Stott – he was as straight as his putter, as honest as the crease in his trousers and with just enough eccentricities to make him unforgettable.

'Iain Anders as McVitie was just a fantastic character,' says James Macpherson. 'There is a trend in modern television for everyone to be good-looking and young, but there is a lot to be said for the snobby McVitie, who wasn't quite a cartoon character but who was slightly weird.'

He certainly wasn't a typical sort of boss. His staff always had a pretty free rein underneath him, and he would generally only

Anders provided a much-needed sense of continuity.

really get involved if the case impinged on someone from his golf club. As time went on, he noticeably mellowed, at times becoming the provider of light relief, such as his appearance in a fancy-dress Chinese mandarin outfit in 'Flesh and Blood' (1989).

In later years, after McManus died, his presence provided a much-needed sense of continuity. He also showed a human side, as when Colin McCredie's character, Fraser, is revealed to be gay in 'Angel Eyes' (1996). Unexpectedly, perhaps, it is he who takes the liberal view, telling the more concerned Jardine to 'unbutton it'.

McVitie had an on-screen heart scare in 'Prayer for the Dead' (1995), but Iain missed the first non-McManus *Taggart*, 'Black Orchid' (1995), due to real-life ill health – his place taken by Julian Glover as Superintendent Drummond.

His death of a pancreatic illness at a Sussex hospital in June 1997 was greatly felt by his colleagues on *Taggart*. 'Iain Anders was just the most wonderful actor,' recalls Glenn. 'I remember him saying to me, "I'm happy as long as I can come along and have a dozen good scenes; I just don't want to be some boring superintendent who barks out instructions from behind a desk."'

He was never that.

Blythe Duff has starred in *Taggart* as DS Jackie Reid for seventeen years. She is the programme's longest-serving member of the cast and, in the audience's mind, an important link with its earliest days. In fact, to many, Reid *is Taggart*…just better-looking.

Blythe Duff grew up on a council estate in East Kilbride. Her parents blessed her with optimism from the beginning, naming her after the well-known birthday rhyme 'The child that's born on the Sabbath day is bonny and *blithe* and good and gay.'

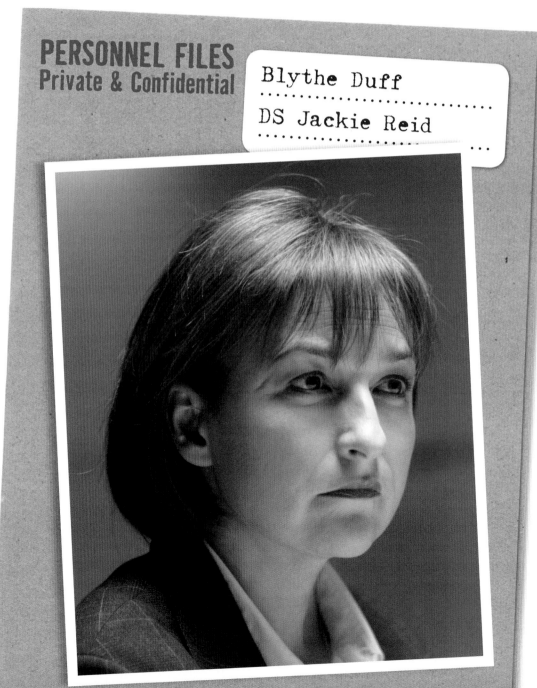

PERSONNEL FILES
Private & Confidential

Blythe Duff
DS Jackie Reid

'The name did cause quite a lot of confusion,' the actress comments. 'On the first day at school the teachers didn't know if I was a boy or a girl. Well, until they saw me.'

Blythe left high school amidst the depths of the 1980s economic recession determined to be an actress. She took a job on a Youth Opportunities Theatre Scheme paying her just £25 a week and toured all round Scotland. Blythe also tried out for the RSAMD but failed the audition three times, being told to get more experience. She did, however, win a £600 grant from the Prince's Trust, which allowed her to join a Scottish Youth Theatre residency course.

It was an uphill start to a career and one she's not forgotten. Over the next few years she found regular work in the Scottish theatre and now repays the faith showed in her by donating some of her spare time to being a patron of the Scottish Youth Theatre and as an ambassador for the Prince's Trust. She also takes stage roles when her *Taggart* schedule allows, including the launch of the National Theatre for Scotland in 2006.

By the time she was twenty-eight Blythe had gained enough experience to turn Robert Love's eye at a production at the Tron Theatre in Glasgow, where she was playing a strong-willed daughter in a play about a Scots-Italian family. 'She was unusual, not conventional-looking, but distinctive. She gave a very powerful performance,' Robert recalls.

The prospect of a significant role in Scotland's biggest TV export at the time was daunting, but it is typical of her down-to-earth approach that she started on the show while giving herself a major reality-check: the persistent rumour across Scotland at the time was that *Taggart* wasn't long for the axe.

Blythe recalls her first awkward days on the job filming 'Death Comes Softly' (1990). 'I literally had to be walked through it,' she says. 'It was "Oh, my God, what do I do now?" James was an absolute star, though. He showed me how to pace out a scene. He became my link with the programme and showed me how I could fit in.'

The follow-up, 'Rogues' Gallery' (1990), saw Reid 'seconded' to CID and in plain clothes for the first time, but her promotion wasn't straightforward. Jim Taggart wasn't the problem – the old softy ended up treating her better than his own daughter – the issue was her driving.

'The script called for Reid to be Taggart's driver, but I hadn't passed my test,' Blythe explains. 'I've still got the offer letter. It said, "If you fail your driving test, this contract will not be binding." It was a hard thing to sit my test while filming my first *Taggart* and thinking, "If I don't pass, I won't be able to act any more. It should be about my acting, not my driving!" I had four hours of lessons each day but still managed to fail. I got a second test after we'd started filming and fortunately passed.'

> 'The script called for Reid to be Taggart's driver, but I hadn't passed my test.'

When Mark McManus died, Blythe became the programme's co-lead with James Macpherson. The enhanced status increased her celebrity, but living and working in Glasgow has allowed her to live a relatively normal life.

'I don't hide; I enjoy speaking to people,' she says. 'There are only a few occasions when I don't want to – at a funeral, perhaps, or in a hospital. Those are the sorts of times when I don't particularly like being on telly. But Dawn French once said, if you want to be anonymous you can be; if you don't, you don't have to be. It's a way of walking about and not taking everyone in.'

Away from the screen, Blythe enjoys family life in a village on the outskirts of Glasgow with her husband, Tom Forrest. 'At work, I'm Blythe Duff, but elsewhere – at the children's schools, for example – I'm Mrs Forrest,' she says. 'Never Blythe Forrest, though, that sounds like an air-freshener!'

Her marriage to Tom in 1998 made headlines. He was a widower with two young girls, Katie and Sarah, aged four and two, and he'd lived next door. Blythe had bought the property next to his from her sister some two years after Tom's wife, Aileen, had died. Blythe had just split from the actor Moray Hunter after a three-year relationship, and she first became friends with Tom and then soul mates. For the newspapers, the fact he

For a nervous Blythe Duff the role of Jackie Reid depended on passing her driving test.

was a detective sergeant with the CID in Glasgow just made it all the better. 'They said we couldn't fight at home because we were the same rank,' laughs Blythe.

The union has been an extremely happy one. 'I've always had a fantastic set-up and Tom's a fantastic father; he's always been there for the girls,' she says. 'They've a fantastic grandmother, fantastic auntie and loads of support, and people who have always been there for them, and so when I came on board, I thought, "This is going to work: this is what I want, this is what Tom wants, this is going to be fine." I always knew the bottom line was that Tom is going to be their dad and that he would get them through it.'

Blythe relaxing at home. 'Yes, it *has* been a hard day at the office, dear.'

Tom resigned from the police force after twenty years' service in 2003 to become a property developer. 'We were in the fortunate position that we could afford for him to leave,' Blythe explains. 'And there's only one person you can have on a murder at any one point in the house, do you know what I mean? Without wanting to sound churlish, when he'd phone me to say, "I've got a murder on, darling," you just felt…' She lets out a groan. 'In real life, police work takes you away – they work round the clock until a case is sorted.'

Tom proves to be invaluable, however, whether it is as a personal bodyguard or as a stand-in for Alex Norton, Colin McCredie or John Michie. 'He goes through my lines with me the night before I work – he's played all the other characters over the years. He'll also go, "Nah, that's no' right," if something is inaccurate. A lot of the problems are because Scots law can be different to English law; that's where we come a-cropper most of the time. We do have a police adviser, but sometimes it is just easier to ask Tom – well, for me it is.

'He likes actors and he understands the business, but he doesn't want to be in the business,' says Blythe. 'He's happy to go to the dos with me, and he knows when to step in and shield me when I need it – he's six foot five inches and people don't really mess with that.'

At work, Blythe admits playing 'mother hen' to a cast dominated by 'boys', often telling them off for putting their feet up on the seats of the Winnebago or not returning a dirty plate. But there's a sense this is partly because she feels so protective of *Taggart* as a whole.

Blythe remains one of the show's main pillars – popular with the audience, who readily associate with Reid's sense of justice and seen-it-all, still-appalled approach.

'There's only one person you can have on a murder at any one point in the house.'

John Michie
....
DI Robbie Ross
....

Born in Burma, raised in Kenya and educated in one of Scotland's most exclusive schools, the odds were against John Michie finding a career as a TV copper, but the actor playing *Taggart*'s occasionally dodgy DI, Robbie Ross, has taken to the mean streets of Glasgow like a natural.

John Michie's father came from Balfron in Perthshire and became a banker. 'He'd rather have spent his life in the Scottish countryside, but money is money,' observes John. 'There were no jobs at home, so he ended up in India with a bank.'

John was born in 1956, in Burma, the second of three children. His parents had met a few years before at an Indian hospital, where his mum was a nurse and his dad was suffering a nasty case of jaundice. It was love at first sight.

The family settled in Kenya, and it was the White Highlands rather than the Scottish ones John knew until he was twelve, and where he learned how to speak Swahili. 'It is a beautiful part of the world,' says John, 'but we moved back to Edinburgh and I went to school in Scotland.'

John was sent to Glenalmond – Perthshire's exclusive boarding school – around the time a disgruntled Robbie Coltrane was leaving. At the time the school had a reputation for being traditional and conformist with a regime made up of rugger, cold baths, plenty of discipline…and no girls.

'I found it difficult at first, but I actually got into it. I think you can either kick against a school like that or go with it, and I decided to go with it. And really it's a beautiful place,' he explains. 'I'm sure that's where I got my love of the hills. If I have a day off here, I go and climb a Munro and get away from the madness of the set.'

John recalls visiting the theatre as a teenager and being thrilled on a trip to London by seeing Glenda Jackson in *Hedda Gabler* and *The Rocky Horror Show*, but unlike his co-stars, he didn't take to the stage until much later.

'No, I never wanted to dress up as a girl to do Gilbert and Sullivan,' he laughs, referring to the types of production the school would put on in those days. Instead, he left Glenalmond and took a year out – travelling to Australia by cargo ship, where he eventually worked as a cattle herder. On his return to the UK, he signed up to study law at Bournemouth Polytechnic.

'I realised it wasn't for me and I came back to Edinburgh,' he says. 'I worked in some bars and got a job as a stage hand at the Traverse Theatre. I kind of thought I would slip into acting through the back door when no one was looking. I'd already had two years of grant money so I had no funding to go to drama school. Eventually, I got an Equity card and got a job in a theatre in Nairobi. That was my training ground, really. I did a lot of plays there.'

It wasn't long before he returned to Britain, however, in 1984, settling in London, where he got a bit-part in *A Passage to India* before landing a significant role as a cheeky Scottish market trader in ITV's soap venture *Albion Market*. Although the show's demise was disappointing to him, the rapid turnover of episodes gave him invaluable experience for the television work that followed.

Between 1985 and 1998 John appeared in *Casualty*, *Lovejoy*, *Poirot*, *Rockcliffe's Babies*, *Moon and Son*, *Bugs* and *Heartbeat*, to name but a few.

'I kind of thought I would slip into acting through the back door when no one was looking.'

There was a major role in *London Bridge* – a London-based soap, which amassed a cult following on late-night ITV – and a cheeky performance in *The Bare Necessities*, another ITV drama, about a group of miners who turn to stripping to make money. 'I never could understand why that didn't do better,' he reflects. 'It was the same idea as *The Full Monty*, but came out before the film did.'

Looking at his CV, you realise John's career was ready to leap forward, and by the time he won the part of DI Robbie Ross in *Taggart*, he'd just finished two films. The likeable British production *Monk Dawson* saw John in the role of a troubled priest and featured one of the funniest out-takes of all time. When he runs out of communion wafers when he's not supposed to, John leans down to the extra and tells her, 'Sorry, darlin', but we're out of the bread.'

To Walk With Lions featured Richard Harris as real-life animal conservationist George Adamson – first made famous in *Born Free* (1966).

Filmed in familiar Kenyan surroundings, Michie played a young drifter, Fitzjohn, who arrives at the sanctuary fleeing a run-down town where he had started a fight. He grows attached to Adamson and tries to encourage the octogenarian to leave the country, where the government and various other interests want to shut down his lion sanctuary. Stubbornly, George stays put and is ultimately murdered. With this recent experience, John arrived on the set of *Taggart* full of confidence.

Ross was introduced in 'A Few Bad Men' (1998) and immediately marked down as a potential troublemaker by the newly promoted DCI Mike Jardine. Reid and Fraser look on with some amusement, wondering whether the rakishly good-looking newcomer – who clearly fancies himself – will last the distance.

'It's a great, fun character to play because he's so flawed,' John says. 'He is a bit of a wild card and follows his instincts and hunches so full on that he sometimes hits the jackpot.'

John met his wife, Carol, in the early 1990s when she was working as a choreographer. 'It was a Walkers crisps commercial – I was eating the crisp and she was doing the choreography,' he explains. A former dancer with the *Top of the Pops* group Hot Gossip, Carol was responsible for teaching an entire generation of pop stars how to dance. John and Carol now have three children – Daisy, Sam and Luella.

'I usually rent a flat in the West End of Glasgow during the week when we are filming, and I fly down to London at weekends,' he explains. 'The kids are at school down there, and my wife's life is down there, so it doesn't make sense for us to move.'

He likes to keep active in his local community and has a wide range of interests. While his wife serves as a governor of their local school, he works

'It's a great, fun character to play because he's so flawed.'

regularly with the Islington Youth Theatre. He is keen on yoga and hill walking – preferring a hike to going to watch a football match as leisure.

But are his children fans of the show?

He chuckles. 'They don't watch it. To be honest, I don't make a big deal of it, because being on television isn't a big deal, it's a job. But I remember one night my wife was out and I was in on my own and they were all upstairs and there was a new *Taggart* on, so I called up, "Daisy, Sam, Luella, the new *Taggart* is on. I'm turning it on now whoever wants to see it…"

'I got no response. It was halfway through when my eldest daughter finally walked in. She looked at me watching myself on the telly and just said, "Oh, bless."'

PERSONNEL FILES
Private & Confidential

Robert Robertson
....
Dr Stephen Andrews
....

For seventeen years Robert Robertson was *Taggart*'s gentle giant, Dr Stephen Andrews – the pathologist who never misled the detectives with a hasty conclusion or half-baked supposition.

'Double Bob', as he was nicknamed, was a popular figure on set, genial and fun, with a wicked sense of humour. Born in St Andrews in 1930, he began a long stage career at the Manchester Rep in 1948. In London's West End he played Dr Grimwig in the musical *Oliver!*, and wrote and performed his own one-man show, *Your Humble Servant*, at the capital's Open Space Theatre.

In 1973 he returned to Scotland for a stint at Dundee Rep, returning three years later as its artistic director, a role he was to keep until 1992.

His stage roles included Willy Loman in *Death of a Salesman*, Big Daddy in *Cat on a Hot Tin Roof* and Bottom in *A Midsummer Night's Dream*. He directed plays such as *The Importance of Being Earnest* and *The Cherry Orchard*, working with a wide range of actors and actresses, including many of his fellow *Taggart* cast members and the likes of Joanna Lumley and Sandy Morton.

With his kind eyes and his pipe seemingly permanently located in the corner of his mouth, Dr Andrews was the team's friendly uncle, once removed from the rank hierarchy of the police force but indispensable when it came to studying a crime scene.

His first appearance came in *Killer*, the *Taggart* pilot. In his trademark Barbour jackets, he was always the first person the detectives turned to at the scene of a crime. Understated and never anything but real, his performances were nevertheless shot through with a sense of whimsy that brought his necessarily technical dialogue to life. He observed the difficult relationships of his colleagues with the same distance and care he brought to a dead body. He always claimed playing a pathologist was anything but typecasting as he had a horror for blood. This being *Taggart*, however, he saw plenty of that over the years.

Robert appeared in fifty-one episodes (including the pilot) – only missing one show due to ill health. While there were other roles on television – a *Dr Who* (1971) and *Day of the Triffids* (1981) and a part in Lars von Trier's cinematic tour de force *Breaking the Waves* – it is as Dr Stephen Andrews that most people will remember him.

Perhaps it was inevitable, considering his prolific theatre career, that he should have fallen ill on stage. During a performance of Robert Burns's *Holly Willie's Prayer* in Perth, January 2001, 'Double Bob' suffered a heart attack and died a few hours later in hospital. A sad ending for a much-loved man, still just seventy years old.

Dr Andrews was the team's friendly uncle.

Harriet Buchan
....

Jean Taggart
....

Never mind the murders, the knowledge that his wife, Jean, was waiting for him at home with a bone to pick or a point to make was reason enough for Jim Taggart to stay out working all hours.

It needed a strong personality to stand up to Jim Taggart, and Harriet Buchan's character provided it. Their relationship, as Glenn Chandler puts it, was all about 'conflict and tension'.

Buchan trained at the Royal Academy of Music in London and worked as a music teacher until suffering acute laryngitis. She then took up acting, but in 1981 was diagnosed with cancer of the left vocal cord. Jean Taggart was her first role after getting the all-clear, and she commented later that suffering a chronic illness had helped her master the role of wheelchair-bound Mrs T.

'People who have had chronic illnesses, like myself and Jean, do have a certain look,' she commented. 'It's different from that of a hale and hearty person.'

Despite her disability, Glenn Chandler was at pains to always make Jean a positive force. She refused to let her handicap stop her from going on holiday or to the theatre or even from running for Parliament, as we saw in 'Hostile Witness' (1990).

'It was a by-election and she was campaigning for more rights for the disabled,' Glenn laughs. 'Taggart was so busy working he got to the voting booth five minutes after it had closed, even though Jean was counting on his vote.'

Indeed, Jean saw no limits to what she could achieve. Sometimes her exploits brought a blush to the chief inspector's stony pallor: her book *Sex and Disablement*, for example, was a bit too frank for a wee laddie like him to cope with. But as a result, she became an inspirational character to many viewers.

Off camera, Harriet Buchan's relationship with Mark McManus could be difficult, too. While filming in Germany for 'Double Jeopardy' (1988), the cast were due to be ferried from one location to another by bus. Somehow, Harriet got waylaid, causing the bus to be rerouted to go and fetch her. Glenn recalls Mark, rather impatiently, declaring she was 'mist in the mountains, mist in the heid'.

'They certainly seemed to spark off each other in the wrong way,' Glenn says. 'It came out in the scenes between them and gave them an edge, but I don't think they were the most pleasurable scenes we ever did.'

Yet there was affection, too. In the 1995 documentary *Mark McManus: the Taggart Years*, Harriet, whose son had been unwell, spoke of Mark sharing his concerns over Marion's cancer. He'd told her, 'All those people outside think we've got everything, and look at us. If only they knew!'

When Mark McManus died, Harriet returned for one last appearance as Jean, in 'Black Orchid' (1995), when her chat with Detective Sergeant Reid is interrupted by a call from the station.

'They've found a body in the Clyde,' Reid tells her.

'Jim's probably there already,' the long-suffering widow replies.

Harriet no longer acts, but takes psychophysical voice workshops.

> 'People who have had chronic illnesses, like myself and Jean, do have a certain look.'

PERSONNEL FILES
Private & Confidential

Mark McManus
....
DCI Jim Taggart
....

As a teenager, Mark McManus used to bunk off work on the Clyde docks to spend the day watching movies. But he had to travel to the other side of the world, to Australia, to discover that his real talent lay in appearing on the big screen. As Glasgow's best-loved stony-faced detective, he found the role he was born to play.

Mark McManus was born on 21 February 1935 in Bellshill, a Lanarkshire mining village near Hamilton, on the outskirts of Glasgow. His family had long lived off the pits, but at the time work was hard to come by and the McManus clan moved around a lot. When Mark left school at fourteen, he initially followed his father, grandfather and great-grandfather down into the mines, but on the encouragement of his parents found work at the docks in Glasgow instead, initially as a timber porter.

This didn't exactly grab him either and he used to slope off to the 'picture house'. It wasn't long before he was looking for something much more challenging. At the age of twenty-two, he left Scotland, along with thousands of his generation, by getting on a boat for Australia, where he travelled before settling in Sydney.

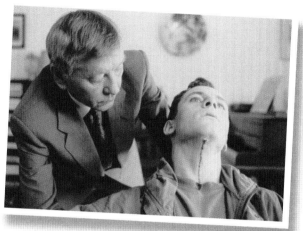

Not long before he died, Mark told writer Geoff Tibballs, 'I lived in a crummy boarding house, run by a stingy Scots landlady whose idea of breakfast every morning was a cup of tea and one frankfurter. There were lots of young lads there – Greeks, Poles, Danes, Italians – and as I spoke her language, I was elected to go and complain. She promised to improve things. And she did – from then on we got a cup of tea, one frankfurter and a dod of tomato sauce!'

Jim Taggart inspects a nasty fatality.

'Lead me to it!'

Mark found work in the Sydney docks, supplementing his income by boxing at the weekend. He collected seventy-two stitches in some twenty-five bouts, deciding to quit when an 'Aborigine giant' rearranged his face almost beyond repair. When he stepped out of the ring, he found himself on the stage.

'There was a sense of romance about the docks [in Sydney],' he told the *Scotsman* in 1983. 'The dockers were wonderful characters, and there were these huge ships sailing in from all over the world…But one day someone put up a notice saying that an amateur drama group were working on a production of Brendan Behan's *The Quare Fellow* and anyone interested should come along. Well, as soon as I stepped on to the stage I just knew this was what I wanted to do. I can't describe the feeling; I just knew it as soon as I started to act. After a week, a producer came to see the show and asked me if I'd consider taking up acting professionally and I just said, "Lead me to it!"'

That was 1962. He spent the next nine years in Australia touring the outback, in everything from Shakespeare – his first professional gig was playing a witch in *Macbeth* – to learning to sing, dance and play the banjo for the Tommy Steele lead role in *Half a Sixpence*. It was an extremely varied period of his life, and one he regularly mined for anecdotes in the decades that followed.

'He was very funny,' recalls Alex Norton, the current *Taggart* chief detective, who co-starred with McManus in 'Knife Edge' (1986). 'Between takes he'd have me in stitches, telling stories about Australia. He once told me he'd acquired a fishing boat and him and a friend were making some sort of living sailing it up and down when one day, underneath them, it was like there was this big sea monster. Like something from the *Pirates of the Caribbean*, this huge, writhing, teeming ball came up and nearly overturned the boat. They landed and told these guys all about it at the pub and everyone ran out. He said that once a year the shrimp congregate into this mass copulation, a huge ball of them together, so all these guys went off to catch the shrimp, *coitus interruptus* if you like.'

Above: For Mark McManus, seen here in 'Cold Blood', acting wasn't always in his sights.
Opposite: McManus, pictured behind the scenes in 'Knife Edge', brought a lot of unexpected humour to the role.

From 1966 to 1970 Mark landed a series of roles in Australian television programmes, including an episode of the long-running television series *Skippy*, where he learned a salutary lesson in the nature of celebrity. 'Mark always told this story about working on *Skippy* and getting his lunch in the canteen and sitting next to a chap with a sack,' laughs Robert Love. 'Then he'd notice the sack was moving and of course it turned out Skippy was in the sack.'

Another highlight was Mick Jagger's film *Ned Kelly*, on which director Tony Richardson encouraged Mark to return to Great Britain, advice he took, arriving in London, along with his Australian wife, Paulette, and their children, Christopher and Kate, in 1971. Over the next few years he was seldom out of work. He joined Bill Bryden's Cottesloe Company at the National Theatre and also appeared at the Royal Court. Notable productions included starring as John Proctor in *The Crucible* and, perhaps surprisingly, as Jesus in a 'promenade' version of the Passion plays – during which he was crucified outside, temporarily causing a halt to traffic on Waterloo Bridge.

Commenting after Mark's death in 1994, the Cottesloe's co-director Sebastian Graham-Jones said, 'His style of acting was exactly what the company was all about. It was direct, uncluttered and unpretentious, and it was very influential.'

Such positive reviews sparked a successful television career. There were episodes of *Colditz* and *Crown Court* in 1973, a recurring part as Harry Carter in *The Brothers*, in 1974, and then the title role in

'As soon as I stepped on to the stage I just knew this was what I wanted to do.'

McManus in 'Violent Delights', 1992.

Sam (1975), a major Granada production at the time about a family of miners in the Pennines, which recalled his own background in Scotland. After that came a part that would help define his future career: the no-nonsense Chief Superintendent Lambie opposite Don Henderson's eccentric Detective George Bulman in ITV's *Strangers* (1980–2), a part he reprised in the 1985 sequel, *Bulman*.

It was this role as a cop that led him to be offered *Taggart*, which gave him a chance to come home to Scotland, where, like the prodigal son, he found himself welcome.

There's a story that McManus decided to watch an early episode of *Taggart* in a Glasgow city-centre bar. All through the show the punters with their pints grumbled and complained about it, so by the end titles he was left utterly dispirited. It was only when he got up to leave, convinced his career was finished, that one of them called over, 'Yer all right, wee man. That wisnae bad. We were just havin' you on.' Apocryphal or not, it feels true.

All of a sudden Mark was a bankable name for ITV and a folk hero at home. Always generous, he was happy to lend his fame to good causes, often fronting charity appeals and campaigning on behalf of Strathclyde Police Force, which accepted him and his gritty on-screen persona as one of their own. There were demands, too, for personal appearances, such as the opening of new cinemas, and guest roles in other television shows, notably Rikki Fulton's sketch comedy *Scotch and Wry* – at the time a New Year's Eve Scottish institution.

The real deal

'He was an absolute gem,' recalls Glenn Chandler. 'I've worked with a lot of actors and he was totally unpretentious and professional. There was nothing standoffish about him whatsoever.'

However, *Taggart* did lead to changes in his private life. As the series was re-commissioned by ITV and his move to Glasgow from England became permanent, Mark split with his first wife, Paulette. Then, in 1990, he married Marion Donald, the show's original wardrobe mistress. Theirs, according to colleagues and friends, was 'undoubtedly a love match'.

'They'd met the first time before *Taggart* on a play, *Two Per Cent*, that we did at STV,' recalled Robert Love. 'As the years went on their relationship developed, though it was quite some time before any of us realised it.'

That was typical of Mark. Away from work, he was a private man who enjoyed life to the full. Although he lived in a flat in town, he also kept a cottage in the countryside for weekend breaks away and he's been variously credited with breeding butterflies as a hobby, owning Clydesdale horses and as a keen yachtsman.

Sometimes it was hard to know where the stories began and reality ceased. With a storyteller's knack of blurring fact and fantasy, he would often entertain journalists with tales that had little to do with real life. In one interview, he declared he'd quit *Taggart* to sail round the world, while in another he'd give a lurid tale of being mugged, or of his car being stolen, even though he didn't drive.

In the main, this was a symptom of Mark's drinking – widely known but seldom reported. Holding his booze was almost certainly a habit he developed on the docks in Scotland and Australia, and a skill that was fine-tuned as an actor. James Macpherson recalls speaking to one actor who'd known Mark during his days at the National Theatre and his account of the wee man who could drink anyone under the table, 'slow and steady'.

When Blythe Duff joined the show in 1990, she recalls 'the word' among Scotland's tight-knit television community was that *Taggart* wouldn't be long for the axe, the lead's problem with the bottle given as the cause.

His last years on *Taggart* saw a physical decline that was distressing to those close to him. But while alcohol was certainly the original source of his ill health, it was exacerbated by a series of personal tragedies. Over a period of just two years he lost his mother and two sisters and then, in October 1993, Marion lost her own two-year battle with cancer.

After her funeral, Mark took a holiday in Australia with family to recuperate. Robert Love recalls being told that Mark arrived down under with no luggage – just a book to read and a change of underwear. 'The weather's hot here, so what else do I need?' is what the actor is said to have told his bemused brother-in-law.

He then returned to Glasgow to film more episodes of *Taggart* in early 1994. However, production of that year's 'Hellfire' and 'Prayer for the Dead', which was shown in 1995, were disrupted by Mark's ill health and reduced abilities. Then, in May 1994, James Macpherson visited him at home and found him a sickly yellow colour. He encouraged him to go into hospital, where he was found to be severely jaundiced. He died on 6 June.

The doctors gave the cause as pneumonia. The papers said it was a broken heart.

Holding his booze was almost certainly a habit he developed on the docks in Scotland and Australia.

Chapter 3

The Show Goes On

Killer won critical acclaim and, more importantly, a large audience, giving ITV the confidence to commission Robert Love to make a further six-part series. The focus would be on Mark McManus's character, and the drama was renamed in Jim Taggart's honour. While the format and cast were mostly unchanged, the classical music that had been a feature of the pilot episode was replaced by a gritty, blues-style theme tune. *Taggart* was relaunched with 'Dead Ringer', broadcast on 2, 9 and 16 July 1985, and was followed immediately by a second three-parter, 'Murder in Season'.

Crew members on the 'Root of Evil' set have fun with a grisly prop.

'Dead Ringer' (1985) illustrated Chandler's developing taste for the grisly and gruesome. It opens not with a murder, as such, but with the discovery of the skeletal remains of a woman in the basement of a house about to be demolished, and the dialogue is as dry as the dirt under the actors' feet.

Taggart:	'We've got a severed leg near the Erskine Bridge.'
Livingstone:	'Human?'
Taggart:	'Naw, the kind you put mint sauce on.'
'Knife Edge' (1986)	

The find reopens a murder case Taggart had long thought closed, and which he discovers was a lot more complicated than he'd ever imagined. No wonder that by the end of the case he is grappling for his own peace of mind – a mental state represented on screen by a peculiar little artefact first introduced in *Killer*.

'Taggart had a little statuette of a Buddha on his desk,' chuckles Glenn. 'I was interested in Buddhism at the time, and I was trying to think of a reason why he would need a new partner. Rather than just be retired, I decided his old partner had gone off to Japan to become a Buddhist monk, leaving the statuette behind as a gift. Jim could never understand why his friend had gone, so he would hold the Buddha when he was puzzling over things.

'In "Dead Ringer", he tosses it away into the Clyde in frustration, only to immediately demand a police diver fetches it back again. The Buddha stayed throughout – we even had a scene after Mark had died in which Jardine finds it in a desk drawer.'

There was a growing confidence, in terms of both plotting and performance. The confrontational relationship between man of the people Jim Taggart and his toffee-nosed sidekick, Livingstone, reached new heights, or rather depths. Early in 'Dead Ringer', Superintendent Murray warns Taggart of his conduct towards his young partner. In response, Jim tells Livingstone, 'When I was a wee boy, my father made me shake hands with my worst enemy…He shook hands with me; I kneed him in the balls.'

'We've been accused of glorifying the cult of the Glasgow hard man,' muses Robert Love, 'but a lot of *Taggart* was about sending that up, and Mark's sense of humour was brilliant there; he'd deliver lines like that totally deadpan.'

'Dead Ringer' featured a strong cast, including Sandy Morton, who was to go on to star as Golly, the gamekeeper, in Highlands drama *Monarch of the Glen*. But it was to be the last time Tom Watson played Murray. A previous commitment meant he was unable to return for the next half of the series, so Robert Love was forced to recast the role, finding Iain Anders as his replacement, McVitie. Murray had been nicknamed 'the Mint'. Taggart immediately branded the new boss 'the Biscuit'.

> **Dr Stephen Andrews (peering at a bone): 'Stunning, a complete pelvic girdle.'**
> **Livingstone: 'Just what you always wanted.'**
> **'Dead Ringer' (1985)**

'Murder in Season' (1985) captures another theme that was to be a feature of *Taggart* in years to come: the class divide. In Glasgow, the middle-class areas are only too close to some of the city's rougher neighbourhoods, and Taggart's Maryhill beat traditionally took in the affluent, academic West End. In this early episode, an internationally renowned opera singer, Eleanor Samson, played by Isla Blair, is caught up in a complex web of intrigue when her husband's lover is found murdered. But this is also linked to a brutal contract murder in a Glasgow pub. Ken Stott, currently starring in SMG's *Rebus*, turns out to be the killer of the piece – a cunning but outwardly respectable GP called Dr McNaughten.

Chandler's script revelled in the gore of the storyline, and the death scenes were gloriously drawn out. Dorothy Paul, a popular figure in Scottish theatre, who played one of the victims, says her daughters still can't look at the actor who 'did her in' (with a hammer) without an involuntary shudder.

It was the next series, however, that saw the coming to the fore of the darker side of Chandler's imagination. Broadcast over three weeks in February and March 1986, 'Knife Edge' guest-starred Alex Norton – now the show's detective chief inspector – as a lonely butcher with the chopped-up remains of a body hidden beside his racing pigeons. Then we learn body parts are being discovered across the city, seemingly at random.

'In the first scene, you see my character in a doocot – he keeps pigeons – and on the way out he steps over the body of a woman wrapped in plastic,' recalls Alex Norton of his character. 'So you know straightaway he's dodgy. Then you see he's a butcher and they kept cutting to him making black puddings, the inference being that he was putting the woman into the black pudding. Sales of black pudding plummeted across the city after that. I think the butchers were getting together to lynch me.'

'No Mean City'

Killer was punctuated by a specially commissioned piece of music performed on tortured violins, but when the Glasgow detective returned as *Taggart*, Robert Love wanted something grittier and more contemporary to play the drama in and out. He enlisted the help of songwriter Mike Moran, an accomplished composer best known at the time for co-writing the 1977 Eurovision Song Contest runner-up, 'Rock Bottom', with Linsey de Paul. Moran came up with the inspired track, which remains the *Taggart* theme tune to this day, and then added some rasping lyrics.

Glasgow's busy Buchanan Street. 'Glasgow is a great place,' says Maggie Bell. 'It's very warm, but it's also very hard.'

The words were flinty, like the show's lead detective, so they needed a singer to match. Maggie Bell had a voice like Mark McManus had a face. She sang like a woman who'd seen it all, lived through it and gone back for more.

Maggie was originally from Taggart's very own Maryhill in Glasgow, but by this time was living in London. She had been on tour with Moran in America and was asked along to his Surrey studios, where he presented her with 'No Mean City'. The song's lyrics immediately grabbed her. 'I thought it was great,' she says. 'I thought it summed up the city very well because Glasgow is a great place; it's very warm, but it's also very hard.' Maggie and Moran recorded the track that same day.

With the theme tune such a popular feature of the show, Maggie's involvement with *Taggart* was to be developed. Robert Love asked her to

appear in the show in 'Evil Eye' (1990) as a gypsy fortune-teller murdered at her home on the banks of Loch Lomond. It was, if you like, *Taggart's* way of saying thank you…the whodunit equivalent of an MBE.

'It took five days to shoot, and Mark McManus was the nicest, most fun man,' Maggie recalls. 'But do you know who came and killed me? It was John Hannah! He was only a young actor then, but it makes me laugh to think I'd been killed by someone who is now so famous.'

Maggie had risen to prominence in the late 1960s and early 1970s performing around Glasgow and in Germany. She met up with the guitarist Leslie Harvey, forming a group called Power, which later became Stone the Crows. Tragically, Harvey was electrocuted and killed during a sound check in Swansea in 1972, and although a replacement, Jim McCulloch, was found, the group split up the following year, with Maggie going solo. McCulloch, incidentally, joined up with Paul McCartney for Wings.

Maggie's album *Queen of the Night* (1974) made the American top ten and she went on tour in America supporting Earth, Wind and Fire. But when playing in auditoriums in the 'deep south' she found that the audience wouldn't react to her at all. Suspecting it might be because she was a white woman playing to an entirely black audience, she came up with the idea of performing her first song from behind a screen, only revealing her identity afterwards. The trick paid off and audiences started to warm to the Scottish woman who sang like a southern soul diva.

Maggie went on to enjoy a British number-eleven hit with B. A. Robertson, 'Hold Me', in 1981, before moving to Holland, where she completely gave up

Glasgow's Argyle Street Bridge. The lyrics of 'No Mean City' perfectly summed up the spirit of the city.

being a singer. More recently, however, she decided she wanted to perform again. 'I thought to myself, "I could be out doing gigs. I'm sixty now, and I could stay here and next thing I know I'm eighty and it's too late, or I could get out and go back to work while I've still got a voice."'

Maggie now performs live with the British Blues Quintet – herself, Zoot Money, on keyboards, Miller Anderson on guitar, bass player Colin Hodgkinson and drummer Colin Allen. 'I'm loving it. There's no pressure. No one is breathing over your neck – no managers or record-company people, nothing. It's been great.'

And since returning to performing, she finds she keeps getting asked to play 'No Mean City'. As she says, 'People love that song.'

'No Mean City' by Mike Moran, sung by Maggie Bell:
Yes, I know the city like a lover.
Good or bad, it's hard to love another that I've found.
This is no mean town, no mean city.

When I'm far away, I long to see ya.
In my mind, I know you'll always be around.
This is no mean town, no mean city.

City life is strange, you take your share of the good times and bad times,
Always something playing on your mind,
Playing on your mind.
It's the only place that I would be willing to die for,
It's the only life I've ever seen.

Night or day, she feeds me like a mother.
Good or bad, it's hard to love another that I've found.
This is no mean town, no mean city.

Yes, I know the city like a lover.
Good or bad, it's hard to love another that I've found.
This is no mean town, no mean city.

City life is strange, you take your share of the good times and bad times,
Always something praying on your mind,
Praying on your mind.
It's the only place that I would be willing to die for,
It's the only life I've ever seen.
This town is so mean, no mean city, no mean city.

'I used to bounce Michael on my knee'

In 1986 *Taggart* was on a high. Ratings were good and the series had been recommissioned for the following year. The signs were that ITV would stick with it for the long haul.

However, Alastair Duncan made it known he would sign on for three more episodes and then quit, as he was eager to relocate to London and try other roles. Livingstone had been at loggerheads with Jim Taggart since the first day they set eyes on each other: their worldview, class background and approach to policing were totally at odds. While their relationship had mellowed – Peter had even been invited back to Jim's home, where he'd bonded with Jean in a discussion about classical music – it was never warm. Livingstone's departure gave Robert Love and Glenn Chandler an opportunity to rethink the show's central partnership.

They introduced Mike Jardine, a young detective sergeant, as 'sidekick to the sidekick' in 'The Killing Philosophy', Duncan's last outing, broadcast in April 1987. The contrast between the two DSs couldn't be more obvious: Jardine was a Glasgow boy and the son of an old colleague of Jim's, cut, essentially, from the same cloth.

In the next *Taggart*, 'Funeral Rights' (1987), although Jardine is confirmed as Taggart's 'neighbour', in order to maintain a sense of friction a clear divide is made between the two men. In a memorable scene, Jardine chats with Taggart in the pub:

Taggart: 'What's that?'
Jardine: 'Mineral water.'
Taggart: 'And nuts? What are you planning to do, hibernate?'
'Double Jeopardy' (1988)

Taggart and Jardine 'enjoy' a drink in 1988's 'Double Jeopardy'.

Jardine reveals he has made two big decisions in his life: he's teetotal, and he's a Christian.

Jim Taggart's feet were too rooted in the muck and grime of Glasgow's more dangerous streets for him ever to think about things like religion. As for not drinking, that couldn't fail to get up his nose. Bad enough that Peter Livingstone used to sip half-pints of lager and blackcurrant, but at least that was alcohol.

'Because Jardine is teetotal, it meant Taggart couldn't even share a whisky with his new partner, and I thought that would really get up his nose,' says Chandler.

Taggart: 'I used to bounce Michael on my knee.'
Livingstone: 'And he survived?'
'The Killing Philosophy' (1987)

Taggartland

With *Taggart* now an ongoing series, Glenn Chandler was determined that it wouldn't become stale. One way of keeping it fresh was to allow his imagination to run riot with the grim and grisly elements of each episode. He began to collect books and magazines on murder and true crime. This raw material was his inspiration for the dastardly plots that were his *Taggart* trademark.

'You have to be like a juggler, keep all the balls in the air and never let it flag,' he says of writing a thriller. 'Agatha Christie used to say if you feel the plot is flagging a bit, bring on a man with a gun. And I used to say, "I'm treading water here…I'd better bump off someone else." I always looked for something different in a good murder, something off beam – it can't just be a shooting or a stabbing. I was attracted to stories that were more exotic than you got in *Z Cars* or *The Sweeney*. Instead of Glasgow villains who own casinos, I was much more interested in the bespectacled accountant with a body under the floorboards, or the femme fatale.'

'Glenn's imagination became more gothic,' says Robert Love. 'We never based our cases on real events – Glenn came up with all the stories himself. I remember when ram-raiding became an issue for a while, cars getting run into shopping malls. People said to me, "Why don't you make a *Taggart* about ram-raiding?" I'd tell them that would be good for a police series, not a *Taggart*. What Glenn liked wasn't a story about organised crime, or a big fraud, he likes something about somebody who is digging in their back garden or what is going on in the villa's basement. Not your average, conventional stuff.'

Certainly, *Taggart* could never be confused with a police procedural like *The Bill* or America's slick forensic-science drama *CSI*. The series stayed true to its original purpose – to deliver a good old-fashioned whodunit, shot through with dark and occasionally off-the-wall humour. The phrase Robert and Glenn used as shorthand to sum up this approach was 'Grand Guignol', a reference to the Paris theatre that, from 1897 to 1962, revelled in tales of grisly, blood-soaked horror, often employing cuts of meat from the local butcher's to provide special effects.

Perhaps it was this Glenn had in mind when he came up with the idea of the severed limbs in 'Knife Edge' (1986), which required him to pacify the concerned

D'ye ken?

Once, Mark got speaking to an elderly woman while on location who asked for his autograph. After chatting for a bit, and it being cold and wet, he invites her into the Winnebago to warm up. Once there, he makes a fuss over her, gets her a cup of tea and a biscuit. She is most appreciative. In fact, she's behaving like he's semi-royalty and can't believe her luck. Then he sits down himself and lights a cigarette.

'Oh, Mr McManus, would you mind not smoking next to me?' the woman said.

The look, by all accounts, would have been enough to get a confession out of any Taggart suspect.

'Right, hen,' replied the actor, 'get oot!'

producer by pointing out, 'The leg will be wrapped up, Robert: you won't see
the end with the blood coming out.' There's more than a hint of the macabre
about John Hannah getting pushed into the pig-feed grinder in 'Evil Eye'
(1990) and in 1987's 'The Killing Philosophy', with its frank depiction of a
man breathing his last with a crossbow dart in his throat. But *Taggart's* flights
of fancy didn't stop at the way people were being killed. 'People say it is a
gritty, realistic series,' says Robert. 'Well, yes, it has a gritty, realistic surface, but
think of some of the stories: there's one called "Gingerbread" [1993], which
starts with a book of fairy tales. It has two children in it who are like Hansel
and Gretel, a wicked witch in a little cottage, like a "gingerbread house", who
makes friends with them by giving them treats.'

James Macpherson similarly considers that particular three-parter a
highlight of the McManus years – and his all-time favourite episode. 'I'd felt

Opposite: Off-the-wall humour and a hint of the macabre in 1988's 'Root of Evil'. **Left and below:** A Hansel-and-Gretel feel for the woodland setting of 1993's 'Gingerbread'.

'Nest of Vipers', 1992. Jim Taggart was no stranger to a snake in the grass.

the previous one hadn't been that strong, but the first page of "Gingerbread" really grabbed you. It read something like, "A woman dragging a body down the stairs with the head bouncing on every step." Now, instantly you are going, "What's this?"'

Stuart Hepburn, who has written a number of key *Taggart* episodes and appeared in the early McManus stories as DS Kenny Forfar, says the secret of the show is that it isn't really set in Glasgow at all, but in a sort of parallel universe. 'Robert was very clever because he realised it wasn't a police series, it was about Taggartland. It had to be credible but not realistic. It was more important that each story had a beginning, middle and an end, rather than it seem like a real police station,' he says.

Only in Taggartland would anyone commit murder with a hand-held crossbow, as in 'The Killing Philosophy' (1987). Only in Taggartland could Annette Crosbie – that sweet, grey-haired actress from *One Foot in the Grave* – play an elderly invalid and yet still go topless, take drugs and murder her husband, as in 'Funeral Rites' (1987). And

Above: *Taggart* has often explored the military world. Behind the scenes of 2005's 'Do or Die'.

only in Taggartland could anyone, least of all Dougray Scott, that nice bloke from the hit US drama *Desperate Housewives*, attempt a series of murders using snakes, as in 'Nest of Vipers' (1992).

The *Taggart* backdrop may have more than a touch of the surreal about it, but, as Stuart Hepburn adds, *Taggart* strikes a chord because the characters seem utterly real. 'Mark McManus used to say every police station in Glasgow seemed to think they had a Taggart. Glenn Chandler invented Taggart out of his head – he was very much a fictional character – but there wasn't a cop shop that didn't have a guy they thought Taggart was based on.'

As the show evolved, Robert Love and his successors today, Eric Coulter and Graeme Gordon, came to realise this idea of 'Taggartland' could be taken further. Each whodunit came to be set in a defined world, a community set apart from the real Glasgow in a way that their detectives

– McManus, Jardine, Reid, Fraser, Ross and Burke – must learn about if they are to succeed in finding their killer.

Choosing this 'world' became key to each *Taggart* mystery. In 'Do or Die' (2005) and 'A Few Bad Men' (1998), the world is the military; in 'Black Orchid' (1995), it is the theatre and showbusiness; in 'Hellfire' (1994), it is a world of cults and satanic ritual;

'Out of Bounds' (1998) is about an all-boy boarding school; 'Compensation' (2004) is set in the financially pressured world of modern farming; and 'Users and Losers' (2007) is about a series of murders linked to horse racing.

This feature of *Taggart* is distinct to most other television whodunits and offers fresh challenges to the detectives each episode. Now central to the way each *Taggart* is conceived by the writers and production team, it is part of the reason why the series has been able to sustain such high standards for so long.

Above: Studying the form. The *Taggart* team at the races for 2007's 'Users and Losers' **Opposite bottom:** Cults and satanic ritual made 1994's 'Hellfire' a visual feast.

D'ye ken?

This approach has led to some of the greatest episodes of *Taggart* over the last quarter of a century: it has given us everything from snakes in 'Nest of Vipers' (1992) to football in 'Football Crazy' (2000), escort agencies in 'Dead Reckoning' (1998) and scientific research in 'New Life' (2003).

'The perfect *Taggart* is one that will take you into another world and let you see how other people live,' says Alex Norton.

A woman's touch

By the end of the 1980s *Taggart* needed some new blood. Few police series at that time had featured women cops – the profession was still overwhelmingly a male pursuit, especially at detective level. But women were slowly becoming more prominent, and executive producer Robert Love decided *Taggart* should reflect that.

Above: With women cops few and far between, the sharp and outspoken Reid was soon promoted to detective.
Right: Blythe Duff made her first appearance in 1990's 'Death Comes Softly'.

Love spotted Blythe Duff in a play at Glasgow's Tron Theatre and in 1990 cast her in the role of WPC Jackie Reid, in the three-parter 'Death Comes Softly'. From the start Love and Chandler, who wrote the script, intended Reid to be a significant character.

'Death Comes Softly' opens with the discovery in a tenement flat of the body of an elderly man, played by Russell Hunter. He has been dead for over a week and his corpse is being eaten by flies. It's a grisly opening that sparked much discussion between Dr Stephen Andrews and Jardine about the smell and how quickly maggots develop from larvae.

WPC Reid is the area's beat copper and recalls meeting the deceased. From the beginning she has the nerve to speak up in front of the prickly Jim Taggart, so although she is in uniform, there's no doubt this is a detective in waiting. She also exhibits the dry sense of humour and steely determination that will enable her to hold her own, gaining respect from her male colleagues as a diligent, sharp member of the team in the face of an ever-sceptical boss.

Not that Blythe was counting any metaphorical chickens. 'It was always talked about in the business in Scotland that *this* is the last *Taggart*,' recalls Blythe. 'Whenever you did the series, you assumed it was the last one. That's what television is like – you thought, "The show might come back, but my character might not." So I don't suppose I was ever thinking, "This is a job for seventeen years."

Reid:	'And I spoke to a neighbour three doors up. She said that Mr Scott had a visitor a few weeks back.'
Taggart:	'They notice some things round here, then. Well?'
Reid:	'A big man with a beard, wore a naval-type blue blazer with a badge.'
Taggart:	'Is that all?'
Jardine:	'It's a good description, sir.'
Taggart:	'Sounds like Captain Pugwash.'

'Death Comes Softly' (1990)

'It was an important drama at the time, but interestingly, I hadn't watched it until I was in it,' she adds. 'The majority of actors working in the theatre don't watch television, because they are out in the evenings.

'But I had a sense of the dynamic of it. I knew I was coming in to something that was very established. That's quite an interesting thing to do – you know what you are getting involved in and you see the order of things and how you are going to fit into that. But it is also quite hard to come in to something established where the pressure is on you.'

A hint of attraction between Jackie Reid and Mike Jardine was added to the mix – they even hold hands at one point, though this is only to make two girls stalking Jardine believe they are a couple. Their 'romance' turns out to be one of the programme's longest-running red herrings.

Reid provided another dimension for Glenn Chandler and the other scriptwriters. She was the perfect foil for Jardine – two youngsters having to cope with 'the old man's' rages, while

Jim Taggart is not amused, but Reid finds it hard to suppress a smirk.

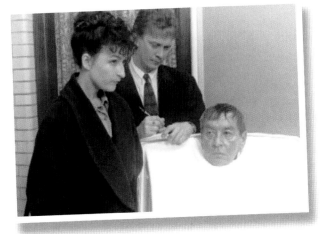

Right: Greg Wise. Ruthless killer? Or Reid's love interest? **Opposite:** A moment's quiet contemplation for the busy detective in 2005's 'A Death Foretold'.

carrying out the spadework on investigations. Never less than competent and extremely hard-working, Reid's half-smirk would often raise a chuckle. In Blythe's own favourite McManus episode, 'Fatal Inheritance' (1993), when confronted with the vision of Jim Taggart soaking in a health spa's mud bath, what she does with her eyebrows is just as funny as Mark's eye-rolling.

Her light comic touch is also put to good effect with the dog scenes in 'Gingerbread' (1993) – a hilarious sequence during which Reid has to follow a dog over several miles to discover where he dug up a human hand.

Also, Reid could handle situations the brusque men could not, while having a vulnerability they didn't possess – as is seen in 'Hellfire' (1994), when she accepts a mission to 'honey-trap' a murder suspect, played by Greg Wise. The audience is never quite sure whether the handsome young bachelor Wise plays is a ruthless killer or the potential love of Reid's life. She plays the moral dilemma of the situation – falling in love with a man she is investigating – extremely well. Blythe admits to feeling anxious about such storylines now. 'I loved working with Greg Wise, that was smashing, but I still feel a bit curly toes at it,' she cringes. 'I don't know if I like Reid when she has a love interest. I don't know if I quite believe it. I think it is hard for me to pull it off.' But there's no doubt Reid's humanity helped secure her a long-lasting place in the *Taggart* pantheon.

Chapter 4

Glasgow: Taggart's Other Star

You hear it said all the time, and not just by nostalgic ex-pat Scots dreaming of tattie scones while living in Australia: 'I love *Taggart* because it's great to see Glasgow on the TV.' For those who know or live in the city, there are two obvious reasons for this. For one, everyone likes the idea of Jackie Reid walking by their house. And then there's the sheer novelty of witnessing your home town – your shopping centre, the coffee shop you go to, your daily morning traffic jam – on a box so often dominated by the London skyline.

But Glasgow is also interesting to the *Taggart* fans who *don't* live north of the border.

As the series became more popular, filming on location became more difficult.

For Ian Madden, who has directed some of the most visually impressive of the recent episodes of *Taggart*, including 'Death Trap' (2002), it is an urban environment of limitless potential. 'It's a great city to shoot in because you can always revisit places; how and why you shoot them and how it influences the story is infinitely variable. The city is one big canvas to paint on, and you never run out of ideas,' he says.

'Glasgow should be and is a character of each *Taggart* story, or the fabric of it. In most of the city centre, it's hard to find a boring shot because of the hills and the gridiron layout of the streets – you get a lot of interesting geometry. And you get a different feel again if you go to the West End, places like Partick.

'There is something very filmic about Glasgow – it has some quite San Francisco-type streets, and it often looks more American than British. It's more filmable than Manchester or Birmingham. God knows why the show is still running after twenty-five years,' he laughs, 'but the city must have something to do with it.'

One of the few houses not to feature in *Taggart*

Taggart has always been filmed on location, giving its often gothic stories the sheen of realism. In the early days, the location manager was a guy called Joe Miller, who went under the nickname 'Joe Miller Get Tae F***'.

The Glasgow skyline: one of the key characters in 2006's 'The Best and the Brightest'.

'That was what he used to tell people if they started to walk into where we were trying to film,' explains James Macpherson with a laugh. '"Get tae f***!"

'Joe was from Bearsden, so a lot of those first episodes of *Taggart* were filmed around Bearsden and Milngavie. It got to the stage where the comedy show *Naked Video* did a sketch in which an estate agent is showing someone round a house and they are explaining, "And this is the only house in the street where they *haven't* filmed a murder for *Taggart*."'

For Glenn Chandler – who had grown up in Edinburgh and was based in the south-east of England – Joe and other Glaswegian members of the production were invaluable. 'Big Joe had a voice like a foghorn and absolutely commanded attention wherever you went,' recalls Glenn. 'He'd

Glasgow's distinctive architecture is seen in 2007's 'Tenement'.

drive me around Glasgow and show me the great new locations he'd found. I remember him saying to me, "Do you know what a doocot is? No?" So he drove me to Maryhill and showed me the doocot – the pigeon loft – we used for "Knife Edge" [1986]. If we passed somewhere, an old Victorian house for instance, he'd just jump out of the car, knock on the door and say, "Can we use your hoose for *Taggart*?"'

Cheese, wine and alleyways

For a population of just 600,000, Glasgow is a relatively diverse place, a quality the programme has always managed to capture. '*Taggart* is an extraordinary archive for the city,' argues Blythe Duff. 'Glasgow is the star of *Taggart* – it is a cliché, but it's true – because it provides us with such a fantastic backdrop. Something Robert Love did very successfully was show

the cheese and wine aspect of Glasgow combined with the rough side. That's a combination that generally works really well: McVitie sipping sherry, then cut to some low-life in an alleyway somewhere.'

'Death Comes Softly', Blythe's 1990 debut, is a terrific example of the way the city's poor and wealthy rub shoulders with each other. Much of the action takes place in a substantial Victorian townhouse overlooked by a block of council flats. The juxtaposition lasts today and can be seen in the city's Broomhill. But as Blythe points out, *Taggart* represents an extraordinary visual history of Glasgow and it is unlikely that there is a Glasgow landmark that has not been used.

In 1983's *Killer*, the streets look bombed out. Tenement flats have their windows boarded up – they've been vacated, most likely in preparation for demolition. The city was at the time suffering the worst recession in living memory, reeling from the collapse of its heavy industries. Even its sense of identity was under question.

'Shipbuilding, steel, all the support industries, they were all affected. The mindset had been that people went into an industry and they were there for life. Generations of families did their apprenticeship with the same company,' explains Fiona Hayes, Glasgow Museum's curator of social history. 'Suddenly that tradition was going or had already gone and there was big unemployment, especially in places like Maryhill, where *Taggart* is set.'

The *Taggart* team investigate an alleyway crime scene in 'A Death Foretold'.

Above left: The underbelly of Glasgow's Kingston Bridge.
Above right: Glasgow's Armadillo, otherwise known as the Clyde Auditorium.

So *Taggart* began at a moment of great historical upheaval in the city. This is played out in the difficult relations Jim Taggart has with Livingstone – the working-class guy threatened by the younger, educated interloper 'frae' Edinburgh.

But Glasgow wasn't to stay in the doldrums for long. The city council launched a major campaign to attract new business: Glasgow's Miles Better, complete with a smiley-face logo. And by the end of the 1980s the social and economic fortunes of the city were changing for the better, and the landscape captured in *Taggart* reflected that.

There were still elements of decay. The derelict buildings under the Kingston Bridge being used as a brothel at the end of 'Funeral Rites' (1987) are balanced by the following year's 'Root of Evil', featuring a grumpy Jim Taggart getting dragged along to the Glasgow Garden Festival.

'The Garden Festival was staged next to the Clyde in an area that had been used for heavy industry,' says Fiona Hayes. 'It was controversial for a lot of people because they felt it was like "dancing on graves". The fact people had worked there and had lost their jobs was incredibly sensitive.'

Other developments in the city's architecture have been catalogued by *Taggart*. In recent years the city centre has been cleaned up, and many new landmarks have been created. Where there was once blackened stone, there is now honey- or red-coloured sandstone. Indeed, the producers today watch the unveiling of any new building with interest – always with an eye to using it in some dastardly plot or other.

But the city's wealth of Victorian architecture – its parks, tenements, terraces and monuments – has also proven a rich seam for the scriptwriters and directors.

D'ye ken?

The exterior of the police HQ in *Taggart* is the University of Strathclyde's Colville Building on North Portland Street. Until recently, interior filming in the police HQ for *Taggart* has taken place at the former St Andrew's Teaching College in Bearsden, in the north of Glasgow. However, the team is set to move to a new base in 2007.

Show me the way to the Armadillo

Killer (1983) opens with a body on the **Kelvin Walkway**. Later, Livingstone chases down a suspect through the **Botanic Gardens**. In 'Dead Ringer' (1985), a ransom is to be paid in **Kelvingrove Park**.

In 'Knife Edge' (1986), **Kensington Gate** in the West End is where the womanising hypnotherapist Alex Dewar, played by Christian Rodska, lives with his lodger Scott, played by Iain Glen.

'The Killing Philosophy' (1987) has the team searching through rubbish at the landfill site at **Gartcosh**. In the title sequence, **Gardner Street** is the steep hill lined with tenements on either side. The police cars are seen racing to the top of it in the show's former title sequence. It is located in Partick, in the West End.

'Cold Blood' (1987) begins with Diane Keen shooting a man in the car park of the recently opened **Scottish Exhibition Centre**.

Above left:
Glasgow's Botanic
Gardens is feted for
its impressive glass
houses.
Above right:
Glasgow's historic
Victorian Kelvingrove
Park on the banks
of the River Kelvin.

In 'Dead Giveaway' (1988), Jardine jumps the turnstiles at **Hillhead Underground**, before Taggart makes an arrest at the next stop, **Kelvinbridge**.

'Hostile Witness' (1990) sees Jim Taggart meeting an old pal at the newly built shopping mall, the **St Enoch's Centre**.

'Rogues' Gallery' (1990) includes a swish city-centre flat, part of a developing trend.

'Double Exposure' (1992) features **Celtic Park**, with its banks of terracing, years before its redevelopment.

In 'Gingerbread' (1993), Mike Jardine visits **Argyle Galleries** to buy an engagement ring.

The tenement-lined Gardner Street in the heart of Glasgow.

Above, from left to right: Glasgow's Kelvinbridge; St Enoch's Shopping Centre; St Andrew's Suspension Bridge, built in 1856; Firhill football ground.

'Black Orchid' (1995) sees a woman plunge to her death from the **South Portland Street Suspension Bridge** after being hypnotised on stage by the Great Sabina into thinking she is a great swimmer. The bridge also features in 'The Ties That Bind' (2005) as a meeting point between DCI Burke and a lawyer contact, John Ferguson, played by David Robb.

In 'Angel Eyes' (1996), the world of smoky boozers Jim Taggart knew seems a million miles from the glossy wine bars of the city's new gay scene.

In 'Dead Reckoning' (1998), a story of call girls and blackmail begins with a murder in the car park of the **Crown Plaza Hotel** and interiors of the **Malmaison**.

'A Fistful of Chips' (1999) sees Robbie Ross chuck a dodgy minidisk player a 'contact' gave him into the Clyde from **St Andrew's Bridge**, which links **Glasgow Green** with **Adelphi Street**.

In 'Football Crazy' (2000), Partick Thistle's ground, **Firhill**, becomes the home of the fictional Strathclyde FC.

In 'Death Trap' (2002), the **Broomielaw**, under the railway bridge, is where Jardine is thrown into the Clyde and drowns. His killer is chased to the **former granaries** on the Clyde, where he appears to die in a car crash. The granaries have since been flattened and replaced with flats, part of the Glasgow Harbour development. Later in that episode, the **Armadillo** concert venue on the Clyde is the setting for the episode's nail-biting finale.

In 'Fire, Burn' (2002), the front steps of the **Glasgow Royal Concert Hall** are the setting for an elaborate trap for the mysterious blackmailer 'the Taxman'. Filmed with a mixture of extras and real passers-by, the sequence looks utterly authentic. The programme also features Ross and Reid having a chat about the death of Mike Jardine in the **Pret A Manger** on Glasgow's **Sauchiehall Street**.

Below, from left to right: Broomielaw Bridge, also known as The Glasgow or Jamaica Street Bridge, was completed in 1772; the Glasgow Meadowside Granary is on the banks of the Clyde in the West End of Glasgow; the Glasgow Royal Concert Hall was built in the late 1980s as a result of Glasgow's 1990 City of Culture status; Sauchiehall Street – one of Glasgow's most famous shopping streets.

'The Friday Event' (2002) sees the **Templeton Carpet Factory** as the setting for a swish flat owned by an artist – at least a year before the developers actually started to convert it. Fraser and Reid also witness a drugs deal while standing under the railway bridge on **Argyle Street** next to **Central Station**

'Hard Man' (2002) features a dramatic final stand-off that takes place at **Central Station**.

In 'New Life' (2003), a car bomb kills an eminent scientist outside the new **Glasgow Science Centre**.

In 'Bad Blood' (2003), the steep slopes of **Garnethill** and **Glasgow Art School** are the backdrop to a gang feud.

Above, from left to right: Glasgow Art School, designed in 1897 by Charles Rennie Mackintosh in the Arts and Crafts style; now a business centre, the 1892 Templeton Carpet Factory was modelled on the Doge's Palace in Venice; Glasgow's Central Station is the busiest railway station in Scotland; the Science Centre is a major science and technology museum.

In the episode entitled 'Halfway House' (2003), Robbie Ross gives chase amidst the shoppers on **Buchanan Street**.

'An Eye for an Eye' (2003) features **Park Circus** as the setting for a women's health clinic.

'Penthouse and Pavement' (2003) shows prostitutes late at night outside the **Barrowland** music venue.

In 'Saints and Sinners' (2004), both the **Necropolis** – Glasgow's ancient cemetery – and **Glasgow Royal Infirmary** are central to the plot. In the same episode, the restaurant that doubles for Silver, where the murdered

Opposite bottom: Burke confronts the mob in 'Bad Blood'. **Below:** Ross gives chase in Central Station.

lawyer and builder meet for a business dinner, is **Etain**, behind **Buchanan Street**.

'Puppet on a String' (2005) sees Jackie Reid meeting a suspected murderer at the **Hunterian Museum**.

'The Wages of Sin' (2005) sees the team rush to the **People's Palace Winter Gardens** to prevent another murder.

In 'A Death Foretold' (2005), Burke and Reid stop for a coffee in **George Square** – where a café has been built especially for them. George Square is often used in *Taggart*: Mike Jardine used it to meet a contact in 'Death Trap' (2002), and Burke and Reid met some environmental campaigners there in 'New Life' (2003).

In 'Cause to Kill' (2005), a body is found, 'crucified', on a smart walkway on the **Clyde**.

In 'The Best and the Brightest' (2006), **Glasgow University** is at the heart of this story about murdered students. The campus also features in 'Nest of Vipers' (1992).

Clockwise, from above: the Barrowland ballroom is a major dancehall and music venue; the Necropolis is a monument to the religious reformer John Knox and was erected in 1825; opened in 1807, the Hunterian is the oldest public museum in Scotland; founded in 1451, Glasgow University is a renowned centre for teaching and research; George Square – Glasgow's central square and the scene of public meetings, political gatherings, riots, protests, celebrations, and concerts.

D'ye ken?

What makes for a great *Taggart*?
'A terrific story, with something a bit different about it, night shoots, great lighting, Glasgow looking terrific,' says James Macpherson.

Chapter 5

Mark McManus: Heart of Gold

It's impossible to overstate the impact Mark McManus had in his role as Jim Taggart. He remains, for many, the standard by which all other sleuths are set. And in Glasgow, he was immediately given folk-hero status: working-class, flint-featured, Jim Taggart took no nonsense and yet, when it came down to it, he had a heart of gold. Together with Glenn Chandler, the Edinburgh public schoolboy who'd barely known Glasgow before he started work on the series, McManus had stumbled on exactly the right ingredients for a character that embodied the very city he lived in.

'We never had a cross word,' says Duncan of McManus.

'Glaswegians loved him,' recalls Isla Blair, who twice guest-starred in the series. 'When I did "Murder in Season" [1985], there was a real buzz about Mark. I was terribly fond of him. I know he had lots of problems, but there was something terribly truthful and good of heart about him. When he looked you in the eye, you didn't feel there was any acting going on.'

Glenn soon realised how much the actor was capable of conveying without speaking a word. 'I used to over-write his part,' he recalls, 'but I soon learned that Mark could do more with an eyebrow than I could with a whole page of dialogue.'

Mark's star quality wasn't, however, immediately obvious to everyone. James Macpherson, who joined the show as the then Detective Sergeant Mike Jardine in 'The Killing Philosophy' in 1986 (broadcast in 1987), admits he initially had his doubts: 'Now I think he was brilliant,' says James, 'but before I started I thought, "No." It's only when you work with someone you realise how brave they are. I've always been a very safe actor and envied the people who go on stage and fail. That's not for me. I don't want to fail at all. Mark was the kind of actor who could go on and be brilliant one night and dreadful another. That's where the genius was.'

Blythe Duff agrees: 'It took me to work with him to realise how good Mark was. He had the ability to make it seem effortless, and that's a talent. It's like Les Dawson's piano playing – you have to be fantastic at it to make it sound that crap.'

In the early series, Jim Taggart doesn't have to look far for an argument. If he wasn't squabbling with Jean at home, he was grumbling about Peter Livingstone at work.

Yet the actor who played that role, Alastair Duncan, has only fond memories of McManus. 'I loved him,' he says. 'I think at the beginning there was a natural distance between us. A bit like our characters, I came from a different background – my father is an academic, very middle class and part of that stuff on screen was us feeling each other out. But we never had

James MacPherson as Det. Sgt. MIKE JARDINE
Blythe Duff as Det. Con. JACKIE REID
Mark McManus as Chief Inspector JIM TAGGART

Scottish Television plc. Cowcaddens, Glasgow G2 3PR

SCOTTISH TELEVISION

a cross word, and as we went on, the more we liked each other. He was a great storyteller and he'd done so many whacky things.'

In the late 1980s and early 1990s *Taggart* was flourishing – enjoying a ratings peak on New Year's Day 1992 with 18.3 million for 'Violent Delights'. But success masked a troubling issue in Mark's life that would eventually cost him his life.

Covering up the fact he was an alcoholic had long been second nature to the actor. James recalls being puzzled by talk of Mark being in the pub all the time. 'But he keeps telling me he's going to the café,' James had told his wife, imagining his co-star spending the night sipping cups of tea and eating sausage and chips. The café, however, was the Queen's Park Café, a working man's pub on the Victoria Road in Glasgow's South Side, not far from where Mark lived.

'We were never particularly aware of it at first,' Robert says of Mark's drinking. 'It was only latterly – the late 1980s probably – that it impinged on his professional life. He was generally very professional and disciplined, but then things did start to fall apart.'

'He never smashed up a nightclub or went berserk in a bar. His alcoholism was very private,' points out Glenn. 'After the day's filming, we'd all go off to the pub, and for me that was all part of it: I thought it was great, mixing with actors. I never realised how big a problem it would become for him. As the series progressed, I'd look at him and realise he was struggling, but I don't think the audience would have known.'

D'ye ken?

What makes the perfect *Taggart*?
'The best episodes of *Taggart* are the ones with humour because they allow an actor to be much darker,' says Blythe Duff. 'I also love the ones where you get the sense of the murder but you don't see it. Sometimes it's more horrific to hear something but not see it.'

McManus with James Macpherson in 1989's 'Flesh and Blood'.

In truth, people did notice, but they were quick to forgive. 'Mark was a charmer, and he could be dead fly about it,' says James. 'Also, we didn't live in each other's pockets and the drink was…I won't say under control, but put it this way, Hal Duncan [the director on "The Killing Philosophy", 1987] once said to Neil, "Jim is learning to act with Mark today," because Mark had a "cold" – in inverted commas – and obviously the "cold" got worse as we went through the day.

'It got to the stage where if I saw a big speech in the script I knew it would be mine. I'd see Mark doing it, too. He'd say, "I think it's better if Jardine says this."

'Being an alcoholic is like being a heroin addict: he drank to stop the shaking. I remember saying to our cinematographer that I was glad when he'd had that first drink because then there are no more shakes and the scene was better. But he'd said, "It's not, because you lose the eyes."'

'I remember there was one *Taggart* when he was completely off the drink. And it was extraordinary to watch because he was fighting for lines. He was on the button,' says Blythe. 'What was incredible about it was that it was widely known and the press knew about it but they didn't sell him down the river. I think they always thought they got too many stories out of him to bring him down.

'In the latter stages of his life, the last few weeks before he died, Mark invited a journalist into his house. Mark had this terrible battered face because he'd just had a fall, but he let this guy in and made him and the photographer a cup of tea and got them a biscuit. They couldn't believe it. Then he'd tell them some story. He always told a different story.'

As the 1990s progressed, Mark's drinking became a growing issue for Robert Love and his co-stars. While the show still carried the branding of his character, Love recognised the supporting cast needed to carry more of the action, and so James Macpherson and Blythe Duff were steadily given more to do.

'The best advert for not drinking, ever'

Alastair Duncan returned to appear in one last *Taggart*, reviving his Livingstone character for the 1994 caper 'Forbidden Fruit'. 'Marion was still alive then, and, you know, I think at that point Mark knew what the drink was doing to him. I don't want to disparage his memory – he did some marvellous work, and we were friends – but I also don't want to sugar-coat him and say he was something he wasn't: he drank.'

Isla Blair guest-starred in the last episode Mark filmed, 'Hellfire' (1994), a particularly gothic story broadcast at Halloween. The eponymous hero is a peripheral character, with Reid taking centre stage as she attempts to 'honey-trap' a suspected murderer, played by Greg Wise.

After not seeing Mark for a while, Isla was surprised by the change in him: 'He was in a very bad way, but he'd had a terrible year and you wondered how he was coping. Ultimately, I suppose he didn't.'

A photocall for Alastair Duncan's final appearance as Livingstone in 1994.

> '**He was in a very bad way, but he'd had a terrible year and you wondered how he was coping. Ultimately, I suppose he didn't.**'

For those closest to him, Mark's physical decline was traumatic. Macpherson had grown close to what in the slang of the Glasgow police at the time was 'his neighbour'. Not just a friend, Mark was like a member of the family, and godfather to his daughter, Kate.

'It was really hard for James,' says Blythe. 'James tried to be there for Mark, and he was the one who convinced him to go to hospital when he did. It was important to Mark that James was there for him personally, not because he was part of the management. It's probably only now we could talk about it – I could never talk about the alcohol when Mark died, out of respect. Even now I don't feel particularly comfortable talking about it. It was something we were all aware of.'

'The drinking became very, very not funny; it was tragic,' James says grimly. 'Most alcoholics hit the gutter before that because they run out of money, but Mark was never going to run out of money so he drank longer before he hit the crisis. People said to me, the press, that he died of a broken heart. No, not quite. But he was shocked.'

James had called by Mark's flat in Glasgow's South Side to check on him, and found his co-star in a terrible state. Filming was due to start soon on a new episode of *Taggart*, 'Legends' (1995), about a series of murders involving a veteran rock band, but it was immediately apparent the chief inspector wasn't going to make it.

'It's the best advert for not drinking, ever,' says James. 'Believe me, you don't ever want to *not* have a liver. He was yellow. One thing you don't want to do is drink to that excess.'

It was James who took McManus to hospital, where the actor who had prided himself on having the 'constitution of an ox' got his final wake-up call.

'I remember him saying to me, in the hospital, "They [the doctors] say I'll no' be working again." I remember that look in his eyes…He was stunned by that. Then he had kidney failure.'

Mark's death on 6 June 1994 was headline news across Britain and sent shockwaves across Scotland.

'It's a bugger of a first day, Jim'

Mark McManus's funeral took place at Glasgow's Holy Cross Church three days later. The pews were full of colleagues, friends and admirers. Outside, hundreds lined the streets to watch the coffin go on its final journey, and Strathclyde Police provided a motorcycle escort.

'It was extraordinary,' says Blythe. 'I couldn't believe how emotional I was when he died – how public it was, and how it remains so. If you lose a friend or family member, then there will be the odd day when someone will say to you, "How's your mum?" or whatever. But with Mark there isn't a day when someone doesn't say to me, "Oh, Mark McManus." It's not usual to be reminded all the time of someone who is dead. You just don't get that.'

'I had to do the eulogy, the bastard,' James adds with something between a choke and a chuckle. 'I explained the first words Mark had ever said to me. It was on "The Killing Philosophy" [1987]. It was peeing down with rain and we were out filming somewhere down on the Kelvin and he just turned to me and said, "It's a bugger of a first day, Jim."

'The priest said to me afterwards, "That's the first time I've heard that word used in a church – good for you."'

On the same day, on the other side of the world, Alastair Duncan went to a bar in Hollywood and toasted the memory of his old Scottish co-star. 'It felt right somehow,' he explains.

James, too, raised a glass to McManus. 'It was only the second time I went for a drink at the Queen's Park Café,' he explains. 'I went there for one, and then to Rogano's [a bar and restaurant in the city centre]. And then I went home.' He shrugs his shoulders: enough said.

Taggart had lost its lead actor, Scotland an icon, and television a great character. Surely the Glasgow detective series would be quietly wound up…

But Robert Love had other ideas.

Chapter 6

Famous Faces

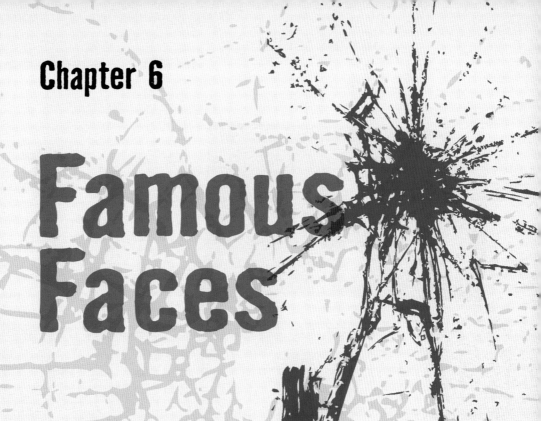

Over the past quarter of a century *Taggart* has played host to an astonishing array of guest stars. Some have been murdered; others have been murderers. Many were big stars when they appeared on the show; quite a few were unknown at the time, but have gone on to great things. Have you seen any of these dodgy characters before?

Opposite: Julie Graham and Alan Cumming live life precariously. 'Death Call', 1986.

Gerard Kelly

Killer (1983) by Glenn Chandler
and 'Mind Over Matter' (2005) by Chris Dolan

Something of a Scottish institution, especially during panto season, if people don't know Gerard from *Mother Goose*, they'll probably recognise him as

Bunny, the demented theatre director in Ricky Gervais's *Extras*. However, older folk will know him from the first ever *Taggart*, when he played unemployed suspect Michael Boyd.

Gerard returned to do a second *Taggart*, 'Mind Over Matter', in 2005, giving a tour de force performance as a murder suspect with severe anger issues attending a counselling group.

Sandy Morton

'Dead Ringer' (1985) by Glenn Chandler

In recent years TV viewers have known Sandy Morton as Golly, the gamekeeper in BBC1's *Monarch of the Glen*. Back in 1985, he was a respected stage actor who'd worked with Robert Robertson's Dundee Rep company when he was cast in the role of David Balfour in this tricky three-parter.

Jim Taggart had put him away for the murder of his wife, but when his wife's body turns up, his conviction is quashed. Balfour is released from prison. However, all is not what it seems and events take an unexpected turn with the kidnap of a nine-month-old baby, Balfour's nephew.

Morton's career has also seen him on the right side of the law, playing cops in *Between the Lines* and *Looking After Jo Jo*.

Isla Blair

'Murder in Season' (1985)
and 'Hellfire' (1994) by Glenn Chandler

Isla Blair played an opera singer under suspicion of murdering her husband's mistress in the early *Taggart*, in a cast that included Ken Stott. Nine years later, she returned to the series for an experience she would never forget. Isla is Lavinia Martin, a wealthy historian whose husband had been brutally murdered some months before. Her son, played by Greg Wise, is the number-one suspect, and in a bid to get evidence, DS Jackie Reid is sent on a 'honey-trap mission'.

Broadcast around Halloween, the episode featured various black-magic references, including a real-life historical document borrowed from Falkirk Museum.

'The joke at the time was that it brought bad luck – and things did keep going wrong,' recalls Isla. 'Small things. But then, after I'd done the scene handling it, I got acute appendicitis. I never did finish filming properly – they had to carefully edit it to look as if I was in scenes I wasn't. It felt like we'd been cursed!'

Still a regular on television, Isla has recently starred in Alan Bennett's *The History Boys* on London's West End.

Dorothy Paul   'Murder in Season' (1985) and 'Flesh and Blood' (1989) by Glenn Chandler

Dorothy Paul is one of the few actors who can claim to have been murdered twice in *Taggart*. In 'Flesh and Blood', she perishes when her country cottage is blown sky high, while in 'Murder in Season', she played a pub cleaner who gets bumped off in a case of mistaken identity – the hit man intended to kill the landlady.

'The actor who killed me was very good – to this day my daughters still look at him sideways,' she says.

Ken Stott   'Murder in Season' (1985) by Glenn Chandler

Ken was a little-known face on television when he played Dr McNaughten in only the second series of *Taggart* to follow the successful pilot, *Killer*. He played a seemingly respectable Glasgow GP who turned out to have designs on his patients' wealth.

Ken has since starred in high-profile TV drama such as *The Vice*, *Messiah* and SMG's current hit, *Rebus*.

Siobhan Redmond, Iain Glen and Alex Norton
'Knife Edge' (1986) by Glenn Chandler

Siobhan Redmond was on her first significant television job when she joined the *Taggart* cast for this classic early episode. She has gone on to have a fruitful career on television and stage, including appearances in *Between the Lines*, *Sea of Souls* and *EastEnders*.

While Alex, now the show's DCI Matt Burke, made black puddings and kept his pigeons happy as the mystery's dodgy butcher, Siobhan

played a journalist on the trail of a sleazy hypnotist.

Iain Glen plays Scott, a drummer in a pop band, who Jim Taggart ultimately suspects of being the murderer. When he goes to arrest him, however, at a nightclub, the real villain shoots Taggart in the back:

Taggart: 'Tell Jean ah'll no make it.'
Livingstone: 'You'll make it.'
Taggart: 'Canada, you dunderheid.'

Iain Glen appeared with Nicole Kidman in *The Blue Room* at London's Donmar Warehouse, and has starred in various films including *Lara Croft: Tomb Raider* with Angelina Jolie and *Beautiful Creatures* with Rachel Weisz and…Alex Norton.

Alan Cumming and Julie Graham

'Death Call' (1986) by Glenn Chandler

Now a star in Hollywood and Broadway, Glasgow's Alan Cumming was a recent drama-school graduate when he landed the role of a suspect in the fourth series of *Taggart*.

In 'Death Call', a trail of macabre murders begins with the murder of the wife of a wealthy landowner, weighed down and sunk to the bottom of a reservoir.

Cumming played a young chemist who comes under suspicion and who is then framed for the crime by DS Kenny Forfar (Stuart Hepburn), an act that costs Forfar his job.

'There was a scene when I was walking backwards next to a viaduct,' Cumming recalls. 'The stuntman had done the bit where he'd fallen off on to the big bouncy thing, but then they took that away when I did it. The stuntman told me count to ten, "then stop and you'll be perfectly safe". Of course, I forgot I had lines to say as well and so I miscounted and I nearly fell. They had to catch me. So now my anxiety dream is that scene, falling off the viaduct in *Taggart*.'

Ayrshire-born Julie Graham played Alan's girlfriend in this story. Now known for the ITV hits *At Home With the Braithewaites* and *William and Mary*, Julie's character had to watch in agony while her lover fell from the viaduct.

Sheila Grier and Simone Lahbib

'The Killing Philosophy' (1987)
by Glenn Chandler

Glasgow-born Sheila Grier was a big star at the time this *Taggart* was made. She'd just enjoyed a busy three-year spell on *Brookside* playing Sandra Maghie, and arrived back in Scotland to play a very 1980s-style femme fatale – all big hair and shoulder pads. Sheila is Kim Redman, a dance teacher who, bored by her husband, starts an affair with a young university student, Patrick.

A young Simone Lahbib.

It becomes increasingly obvious the student (played by Philip Dupuy) is pretty sinister, but is he 'the Glasgow Bowman', who has been murdering Bearsden residents *à la* William Tell with a crossbow?

As Jim Taggart, Peter Livingstone and new boy Mike Jardine carry out their investigation, Patrick attends various seminars, where, sitting behind him each time, is a young Simone Lahbib, who went on to make two other *Taggart* episodes: 'Nest of Vipers' (1992) and 'Prayer for the Dead' (1995). While Grier has enjoyed a career on television appearing in the likes of *Emmerdale*, *Heartbeat* and *Rebus*, Lahbib has had starring roles in *Monarch of the Glen*, *Bad Girls* and as DI Alex Fielding in ITV1's *Wire in the Blood*.

Annette Crosbie   'Funeral Rites' (1987) by Glenn Chandler

You don't normally think of Annette Crosbie stripping off. Whether it is as the long-suffering Mrs Meldrew in *One Foot in the Grave* or as the strait-laced housekeeper, Janet Macpherson, in *Dr Finlay*, she is an actress associated with strict respectability.

That changed when she appeared in the hit film *Calendar Girls* as a senior member of her village WI who agrees to go nude for charity. 'People asked me then if this was the first time I'd gone nude for the camera and I'd said yes, but then I remembered *Taggart*,' she laughs. 'That was the only other time I took my clothes off.'

In 'Funeral Rites', Annette played Maggie Davidson, the acidic but arthritic wife of Paul Young's dentist. As Taggart and Jardine investigate a grisly murder

with overtones of voodoo and black magic, Maggie survives an attempt on her life when an electric heater falls into her bathtub – a scene that explains the actress's nudity. However, things are not all they seem and it takes some clever deduction from Jim to figure it out.

'With *Taggart*, you'd be glued to the set and you'd watch it through and you'd think, "That was great,"' says Annette. 'Then you'd say to yourself, "Now, just how did she know?" And you could never, ever work it out.'

Diane Keen

'Cold Blood' (1987) by Glenn Chandler

One of the most unforgettable *Taggart* openings features Diane Keen – a big name at the time thanks to her hit ITV sitcom *The Cuckoo Waltz* and a string of other television appearances – march through the recently opened Scottish Exhibition Centre on the Clyde, stride across the car park, produce a gun from her handbag and pump six shots into the chest of a man sitting at the wheel of his car. It looks like an open and shut case until Jim Taggart discovers the victim was already dead and that his wife, Diane's character, Ruth Wilson, has something to hide.

Diane Keen has recently appeared in the BBC's daytime soap *Doctors* and drama series *New Street Law*.

James Cosmo

'Dead Giveaway' (1988) by Glenn Chandler

These days James Cosmo is one of Scotland's greatest big-screen exports, a man mountain used to playing key character roles in big-budget Hollywood

movies, be it *Narnia*, *Troy* or *The Last Legion*.

James was a familiar face, if not quite a big name, by the time he appeared in *Taggart* as a suspect in a series of murders using rat poison in food made by Wonderland Products.

'I'm very glad I was able to be in one of the first ones because Mark was still fine and it was very enjoyable. It was an iconic Scottish programme, and Mark was so identifiable with it, it was wonderful,' Cosmo says. 'I'd met him socially a few times, but never worked with him before. That curmudgeonly character so suited Taggart.

'I think if not *every* Scottish actor, certainly *most* have done their *Taggart*. It's like a huge club you belong to. It was easy filming on the street in those days. Glaswegians took *Taggart* to themselves as one of their own. It displayed that flinty aggression and warm-heartedness that Glaswegians always like to portray themselves as. Glaswegians are very proud of *Taggart*.

'I think people just enjoy them for what they are. They've never pretended to be anything other than a tremendous whodunit. It gives you a puzzle, and you wondered how this character, the detective, was going to figure it out. Mark created that iconic character by himself, and just for that he should be remembered very fondly. I don't think there was anyone else around that could have created that character as well as he did.'

Celia Imrie   'Root of Evil' (1988) by Glenn Chandler

A popular actress on television and film, Celia Imrie featured in a classic three-parter set around the Glasgow Garden Festival.

She played Helen Lomax, the matriarch of a family of loansharks who find themselves the targets of a mystery killer.

Celia was already a regular on television with leading roles in *Bergerac* and the Victoria Wood comedy *Acorn Antiques* to her name. She has since starred in TV shows *The New Statesman*, *The Darling Buds of May*, *Dinnerladies* and most recently *Kingdom*, as well as movies *Bridget Jones: The Edge of Reason* and *Frankenstein*. Her most unusual credit is probably for *Star Wars Episode I: The Phantom Menace*, in which she played Fighter Pilot Bravo 5.

Peter Mullan, Ewen Bremner and John Michie
'Love Knot' (1990) by Glenn Chandler

A body is dredged up from the Clyde – a teenage girl. And the murder weapon is most likely a climber's ice pick. Suspicion falls on a Glasgow climbing club, which includes Peter Mullan and Ewen Bremner as members.

Mullan, now a leading writer and director as well as an actor, went on to make award-winning films like *Orphans* and *The Magdalene Sisters*,

and star in Hollywood movies including *Braveheart*, *The Last Legion* and *Children of Men*.

Bremner, who played gormless Spud in *Trainspotting*, has also found success in America with films like *Black Hawk Down* and *Pearl Harbor*.

John Michie, of course, has gone on to star as *Taggart's* own DI Robbie Ross. Here he plays a suspect, Robby Meiklejohn, the ex-boyfriend of the murdered girl, who turns out to be the daughter of an Austrian countess living in the Highlands.

Glenn Chandler had originally conceived this mystery as a second foreign adventure for Jim Taggart and Mike Jardine – following the success of 'Double Jeopardy' a year previously. However, funding from a German television company fell through, and the plot was transferred to the Highlands, though he insisted on keeping the Austrian countess.

Robert Carlyle
'Hostile Witness' (1990) by Glenn Chandler and Stuart Hepburn

Another Scottish actor just starting out on his career, Robert Carlyle, was brought on to *Taggart* to play an ambitious local politician standing on a law and order manifesto in a local by-election. When one of his rivals is murdered, he becomes suspect number one.

Carlyle went on to famously play some of the big and small screen's toughest hard men: Begbie in *Trainspotting*, Renard, the Bond villain in *The World Is Not Enough*, and even the title role in the American mini-series *Hitler: The Rise of Evil*.

All the energy and menace he put into those roles is apparent in the right-wing demagogue he plays in this *Taggart*, filmed the same year he made his first film, *Riff Raff*, with Ken Loach.

John Hannah and Jill Gascoine

'Evil Eye' (1990) by Glenn Chandler

John Hannah had been a contemporary of James Macpherson at drama school in Glasgow, but had mainly appeared on stage by the time he did *Taggart* – four years before the Richard Curtis film *Four Weddings and a Funeral* catapulted him to international stardom.

In 'Evil Eye', he was a young chef who murders a gypsy woman, played by Maggie Bell, the singer of the *Taggart* theme tune (see page 76).

A massive star in 1980s programmes like *The Gentle Touch* and *CATS Eyes*, Jill Gascoine played the role of an adulterous restaurant owner who seduces the young chef.

'The end of the story was on a pig farm, very gruesome,' recalls John with relish. 'I think that was one of the things that made *Taggart* special – it was a gore-fest for primetime television. I met my end in a meat grinder for pigswill!'

Douglas Henshall

'Love Knot' (1990) by Glenn Chandler

These days, Douglas Henshall is generally found chasing prehistoric dinosaurs as time travelling Professor Nick Cutter in ITV1's hit series *Primeval*.

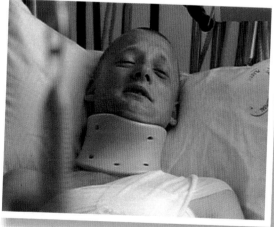

In his career he has played a disparate group of maverick leading men, grieving Michael in *Orphans* (1997), the brooding Levin in ITV's *Anna Karenina* (2000) to the downright mental Dr Daniel Nash in the darkly comic Channel 4 series, *Psychos* (1999), set in an asylum.

Taggart was his television debut – although not exactly an auspicious one. He had just one scene near the beginning of the three-parter, which he performed flat on his back: an unnamed motorcyclist in hospital with serious injuries after a road accident.

David Rintoul
**'Death Comes Softly' (1990) by Glenn Chandler
and 'The Ties That Bind' (2005) by Stuart Hepburn**

After David Rintoul appeared as a suave lawyer in 'Death Comes Softly', he landed the title role in STV's *Dr Finlay*, the revival of the classic series, which also starred Annette Crosbie and helped launch the career of Colin McCredie.

He returned to *Taggart* fifteen years later to play an ambitious assistant chief constable who suspends Burke on a trumped-up sex allegation.

Dougray Scott
'Nest of Vipers' (1992) by Glenn Chandler

These days, Dougray Scott is thought of as the suave publisher in Channel 4's *Desperate Housewives*, or as Tom Cruise's nemesis in *Mission: Impossible II*. But he was another actor *Taggart* producer Robert Love and his team spotted on the way out of drama school and, long before *Soldier, Soldier* turned him into a heart-throb, he was snapped up for what was to be one of the all-time classic three-parters.

Inspired by a news story he'd read about a man getting his pet snake to bite his wife, Glenn Chandler came up with one of the creepiest, most evil plots ever. Snakes are everywhere: in grocery bags, in beds…And the man controlling them is Dougray's zoo keeper, Colin Murphy.

It is the one *Taggart* you don't want to watch with the lights off. 'A villain killing people using snakes…it's not something that happens every day in Glasgow, but that was one of the strengths of the series,' chuckles Robert Love.

Glenn Chandler recalls that Dougray was very concerned with creating a realistic performance. 'He had to live the part,' says Glenn, 'so when he read the script and saw that after Murphy gets arrested he's up all night before being interviewed at eight the next morning, Dougray walked the streets of Glasgow that night, all night. He came in for the shoot looking terrible – he had rings around his eyes and was unshaven.

'In fact, it was a misprint. The time on the script should have been eight p.m., not eight a.m. – the difference between arrest and interview was only meant to be ten minutes. So he'd actually stayed up all night unnecessarily. But it looked great.

'At the end of that episode, there's a scene where Jim Taggart loses control of himself and he launches at him and punches him – because he thinks this guy is a real nutter, a psycho.

'Dougray told Mark, "I want you to hit me, I want this to be real." Mark's like, "I cannae do that, naw." But Dougray says, "Yes." So Mark says, "OK," and he hit him. Dougray fell like a stone. They did it twice after that with a pulled punch. I don't know if Dougray knew Mark was a boxer beforehand – he might not have been so keen to be hit if he had known.'

Michelle Gomez   'Nest of Vipers' (1992) and 'Bloodlines' (1999) by Glenn Chandler

Now known for her brilliant off-the-wall comedy performances as the outrageous Sue White in *Green Wing* and also in *The Book Group*, back in the late 1990s Michelle was an actress working hard to earn herself experience and to win a break.

She'd had a role in *The Acid House*, a film adaptation of Irvine Welsh's book of the same name, and parts in *The Bill*, as well as an earlier appearance in 'Nest of Vipers' (1992) as a hairdresser. In 'Bloodlines', she plays former prison guard Harriet Bailes, lover of Susan Keller, a childkiller recently freed from prison.

Meera Syal and Jason Isaacs   'Double Exposure' (1992) by Stuart Hepburn

Meera Syal was cast as a social worker in this racially charged episode of *Taggart*, but she was still several years away from becoming a household name, thanks to her film *Punjabi on the Beach* and TV comedy hits *Goodness Gracious Me* and *The Kumars*.

Jason Isaacs plays her boyfriend, a suspect in a murder with a perfect alibi: he was filmed in the crowd at an Old Firm match when the crime was being carried out.

He is now best known as the devious Lucius Malfoy in the Harry Potter films, and recently starred in the BBC thriller *The State Within*.

Clare Grogan and Ian Hogg
'The Hit Man' (1992) by John Milne

Clare Grogan first came to prominence as Susan in *Gregory's Girl* (1981) and then in *Comfort and Joy* (1984), but spent most of the 1980s as the lead singer of pop band Altered Images. She returned to acting not long before landing this part in *Taggart*, as the young fiancée of a businessman with gangster connections who is killed in a suspicious plane crash.

The three-parter also featured Ian Hogg, once considered for the role of Jim Taggart himself, as Jimmy Catto, brother of the murdered man, just released from prison, and an old sparring partner of the eponymous detective. When more people are killed, Taggart has to find out if Catto is to blame for the mounting death toll.

Hannah Gordon
'Fatal Inheritance' (1993) by Glenn Chandler

Since the 1960s Hannah Gordon had been a successful and much loved actress on stage and screen. Series like *Upstairs Downstairs*, *Telford's Change* and *My Family and Other Animals* had ensured her status during the 1970s and 1980s as a household name. She'd shown off a fine comic touch in sitcoms like *My Wife Next Door* with John Alderton – confronting the slightly controversial topic of the day, divorce – and guested on Morecambe and Wise's legendary 1973 Christmas special.

In 'Fatal Inheritance', she played Dr Janet Napier, who has been tried for the murder of her husband's mistress, only for the case to be found 'not proven'. Convinced of her guilt, Jim Taggart checks into her health farm to do some snooping, only for another body to turn up, and the case to become increasingly complex.

It includes some memorable scenes, including the sight of the granite-faced 'tec up to his neck in a mud bath. 'That is still my favourite Mark episode,' recalls Blythe. 'I think they had to weigh Mark down in that bath to stop his shorts floating up to the surface. But it really showed what a great sense of humour he could have.'

Daniela Nardini
'Death Without Dishonour' (1993)
by Barry Appleton

Before the cult 1997 series *This Life*, Daniela was a cop in *Taggart* who was given the job of babysitting a woman thought to be a murder target. Daniela didn't do her job very well and the woman ends up being killed.

Peter O'Brien   'Death Without Dishonour' (1993) by Barry Appleton

Peter O'Brien was a member of the original *Neighbours* cast, playing Shane Ramsay, and arrived in the UK after a successful follow-up stint in another Aussie drama, *The Flying Doctors*. He's gone on to enjoy a fruitful career in British and Australian television, with roles in the likes of *Queer as Folk*, *The Bill* and *The Knock*.

In *Taggart*, he arrived as an itinerant piano player looking for a job, and finds himself in luck at a wine bar being opened by Jim's daughter and her fiancé. He's soon stirring things up, however, when young Miss Taggart takes a fancy to him and her father interrupts them mid-snog. 'He's Australian,' she tells her disapproving dad by way of explanation.

Meanwhile, Jim and Mike are investigating the brutal strangulation of an eminent advocate, which appears to be linked to her service with the Territorial Army during the 1990 Gulf War. Could the musician from down under have something to do with it, or is Jim Taggart's suspicion of him simply based on a father's protective instinct?

Derek Riddell

'Prayer for the Dead' (1995) by Barry Appleton and 'Wavelength' (2000) by Mark Greig

Derek shot to prominence as Rab, the repressed homosexual football fan in *The Book Group*, and as commitment-phobe Dr Jamie Patterson

in Channel 4's *No Angels*. But before either of those, he appeared in two episodes of *Taggart*.

In 'Prayer for the Dead' – the last episode screened starring Mark McManus – he played a doctor treating McVitie for a suspected heart attack.

'Yes, but I was also a bigamist and someone was blackmailing me into giving him drugs from the hospital because he knew I was a bigamist,' Derek recalls.

'Then I appeared in "Wavelength", which was about a talk radio station, and I played someone really dodgy who was phoning in all the time. I wasn't the killer, but I was definitely a suspect.

'"Wavelength" meant I got to work with John Michie again – I did my very first job out of drama school with John; we did *Measure for Measure* and *The Real Don Juan* with the Oxford stage company and toured around England for about eight months and we've been friends ever since.

'I still remember watching the very first episode when it was called *Killer*, and I remember liking Neil Duncan as Livingstone, and it felt great to have a detective series set in Glasgow. Mind you, being a Glaswegian I would be a bit worried if there were that many murders really going on in the city. I don't think I'd visit quite as much.'

Derek's currently in America playing a child psychologist in *State of Mind* for Warner Bros Television.

Amanda Redman

'Black Orchid' (1995) by Glenn Chandler

Following the death of Mark McManus, *Taggart* needed to come back with a cracking episode, and 'Black Orchid' was it. ('Legends', which was originally intended to be the next episode was held back for the time being.)

Amanda Redman gave an unforgettable performance as cabaret singer Julie Carson, a woman under the romantic spell of James Laurenson's suspicious hypnotist, Tony Sabina. She even performed the *Taggart* theme tune, 'No Mean City', at the beginning, giving it an unexpected jazz treatment.

Redman was already a well-known actress at this time, but typically of

Taggart, her career was very much on the up when she came to the attention of executive producer Robert Love. She'd starred in one series of ITV's *El CID*, with John Bird, but it wasn't until after 'Black Orchid' that she rose to real prominence in television terms. She starred alongside Ian Holm in a TV version of *King Lear* (1998) before starring in hit series *At Home With the Braithewaites* (2000), the cult films *Sexy Beast* (2000) and

Mike Bassett: England Manager (2001), before leading the cast of BBC1's cop drama *New Tricks*.

Barbara Dickson   'Legends' (1995) by Barry Appleton

Barbara Dickson was a prominent member of the Scottish and north of England folk-music circuit in the 1960s and early 1970s, before making her West End debut in 1975 with the Willy Russell musical *John, Paul, George, Ringo…and Bert*. Her sweet singing voice brought her to the attention of Andrew Lloyd Webber and Tim Rice, who recruited her for their *Evita* album to sing *Another Suitcase in Another Hall*, which went to number eighteen in the UK charts. (Madonna covered it twenty years later, taking it to number seven.)

Further recording success followed. A duet with Elaine Paige, *I Know Him So Well*, from the musical *Chess*, went to number one, and there was success with a series of solo albums. Her profile was kept high with regular appearances on the popular *Two Ronnies* show on BBC1. Other successes included the long-running musical *Blood Brothers* and ITV1's *Band of Gold*.

In 'Legends', the first *Taggart* made after the death of Mark McManus (though 'Black Orchid' was the first to be screened), she is a member of a legendary Scottish rock band, the Adders, who are attempting a reunion tour, only for the lead guitarist to be murdered.

Billy Boyd

'Dead Man's Chest' (1996) by Rick Maher

In one of the more extraordinary guest-star performances, Billy Boyd played Jamie, DS Jackie Reid's autistic cousin, in a yarn about pirates, smuggling and a yearning for high adventure.

It was Boyd's first credited television appearance following drama school, and would help launch him on an extraordinary career. Just three years later he was cast in *Lord of the Rings* as Pippin Took, the hobbit, and the rest is cinematic history.

Incidentally, 'Dead Man's Chest' wasn't the only time Billy appeared in the programme. 'While I was still at drama school, I was asked to be an extra to kiss a girl on a bridge,' he reveals. 'It was me and Jenny Green and it was one of the best kisses of my life.' Sadly, fans will be disappointed to learn that even Billy can't remember the name of the episode.

Brian Capron   'A Fistful of Chips' (1999) by Mark Greig

Brian Capron had been a jobbing TV actor for two decades by the time he cropped up on *Taggart* as Andrew Donaldson, the duplicitous boss of a high-tech computer company.

Viewers of a certain age would have remembered him as 'Hoppy', the sympathetic teacher in the early episodes of *Grange Hill*; others would recognise him from bit-parts in *Casualty*, *The Bill* and *Minder*.

However, *Taggart* clearly did his career prospects some good. In 2002 he was recruited by *Coronation Street* to play Richard Hillman, a seemingly suave, romantic figure who turned out to be a serial killer and the soap's greatest ever villain.

'I had a very fierce comeuppance in *Taggart*,' Brian recalls. 'Someone had the idea that the guy who was beating me up should grab my head and drag me across a glass screen. As he did so, a trail of blood was left behind, and then he pushed me down on a glass table. It was absolutely fantastic.'

Fish

'Skin Deep' (2000) by Nick Doughty

While DC Fraser goes undercover at a gym to investigate a diet pills scam, DI Robbie Ross is accused of accepting a £5,000 bribe. Jardine is left with no option but to suspend him, while Jackie Reid's fiancé, DCI Brian Holmes from Complaints and Discipline, investigates.

Determined to prove his innocence, Ross sets out to find who has set him up, tracing it back to a petty thief, Dougie Todd, who has a vendetta against him.

At this point in the plot, every rock fan watching stands up, plays air guitar and screams, 'Kayleigh!' Because Todd is played by none other than Fish, one-time lead singer of 1980s prog-rock band Marillion.

'It was great to be asked. I think every Scottish actor likes to do a *Taggart* at some time in their career,' says Fish – aka Derek William Dick. 'I was a big *Taggart* fan when it first came out. I was living in London and it was just brilliant to be able to watch something with Scottish accents. That was in the days before Sky Plus or DVD, but when I went touring, people would send the odd episode on VHS.

'My character had this thing about Robbie Ross and was a wife-beater. I had a fight scene with Robbie Ross. We are both big guys and we were going at it like crazy; we even took a radiator off the wall. I think we caused about £1,000 worth of damage by the end, and he caught me one, too. He apologised about it afterwards, though – it was great fun.'

Paul Barber   'Football Crazy' (2000) by Peter Mills

By the time he starred in *Taggart* as Jimmy McEvoy, the manager of the fictional football team Strathclyde FC, Paul (below, right, pictured with Tony Roper) was instantly recognisable as Denzil from *Only Fools and Horses*, as Horse in the hugely successful film *The Full Monty* and from playing Greg Salter in Liverpool soap *Brookside*.

Here the *Taggart* team are on classic ground, as a series of people linked to the club are murdered, with a 'red card' left on each corpse. Barber himself appears a potential suspect in the case – his team are proving to be expensive

flops and he has little to lose – but in the end he winds up a victim.

His end comes in fitting football style: while his blonde dolly bird is in the bathroom slipping into her silk negligée, he swigs back a bottle of vintage champagne, only to find it has been poisoned. Foul, ref!

The Gloved Hand

Numerous episodes including 'Dead Reckoning' (1998), 'Fire, Burn' (2002) and 'An Eye for an Eye' (2003)

For many fans, an episode of *Taggart* without an appearance of the gloved hand is a disappointment. Over the years it has been central to several plots, often appearing to execute the very person you'd just decided was the murderer. In 'Knife Edge' (1986), for example, it is the gloved hand that pumps the bullets into Alex Norton's chest, dispatching the dodgy butcher. In 'Black Orchid' (1995), it claims the life of the Great Sabina's rival hypnotist by crushing him under his sunbed. And it's frequently a star of the *Taggart* pre-title sequence, too. In 'An Eye for an Eye', it sets a booby trap by rigging up a shotgun to fire when an office door is opened.

The glove is, as a rule, black leather, and is sometimes replaced by a heavy boot, as in the pre-title sequence to 'Users and Losers' (2007).

Who is the gloved hand? Arguably the role is even more coveted than being a *Taggart* corpse and only long-serving members of the crew need apply.

Lorraine McIntosh

'Halfway House' (2003) by Stuart Hepburn

The lead singer of Glasgow band Deacon Blue, Lorraine had a successful pop career in the 1980s and 1990s. More recently, she has turned actress, appearing in *Taggart* in 2003 as Brenda Johnstone, the scheming manager of a hostel for the homeless. She has since gone on to star in the Glasgow soap *River City*.

Ashley Jensen

'A Taste of Money' (2005) by Charlie Fletcher

The Scottish actress Ashley Jensen made quite an impact when she guest-starred as a journalist in this tasty *Taggart* about the murder of a restaurant critic – and the brutal, culinary executions that follow.

Jensen's career has certainly blossomed since she joined the *Taggart* team. Her role as Maggie

Jacobs in Ricky Gervais's *Extras* won her a BAFTA nomination and a Golden Rose Award, enough to facilitate a move to America and a starring role in ABC's hit of 2006, *Ugly Betty*, which came to Channel 4 in 2007.

David Bradley
'Law' (2006) by Mike Cullen

David Bradley brought the same cheery demeanour to *Taggart* that has made him famous to a generation of schoolkids as Filch, the miserable school caretaker in the Harry Potter movies. Here he plays a senior member of a travelling community.

Haven't I seen you before?

Below and opposite: Even the lead actors have been seen before. Alex Norton gave a memorable performance as the butcher in 1986's 'Knife Edge'.

Many actors have appeared a number of times in *Taggart* playing different roles:

Bill Denniston did six episodes of *Taggart*, playing a different role each time, including 'Murder in Season' (1985) and 'Ghost Rider' (2000). His oddest credit has to be 'Nest of Vipers' (1992), where he is listed as 'Address to the Haggis'.

Gilly Gilchrist appeared most recently in 'Fade to Black' (2002) as dodgy doctor Adam Gillespie in a murder tale about drugs and obsession.

He'd previously had roles in 'Death Without Dishonour' (1993) as a country and western singer with a secret, and 'Funeral Rites' (1987). He currently stars in BBC Scotland soap *River City*.

John Kay Steel played gangster Raymond Carney in 'Users and Losers' (2007), artist Eddie Drummond in 'The Friday Event' (2002) and a cop in 'Death Without Dishonour' (1993).

James Laurenson has been a murderer twice in the series: in 'Double Jeopardy'

(1988), he did away with a number of his wives, hiding their bodies in buildings he renovated, and in 'Black Orchid' (1995), he was the Great Sabina, using hypnosis to send his victims to their doom. He's since appeared in a wide range of TV programmes, most recently BBC1's *Spooks*.

John McGlynn, a regular on shows like *Doctors* and *Casualty*, has done five different *Taggart* roles: 'Dead Ringer' (1985), 'Evil Eye' (1990), 'Secrets' (1994), 'Long Time Dead' (1999) and 'The Friday Event' (2002).

Brian Pettifer, an old pal of Alex Norton's, has been in three episodes of *Taggart*: 'Funeral Rites' (1987), 'Football Crazy' (2000), as the club chairman Sir Archie Magee, who was murdered under his classic car, and in 'Dead Man Walking' (2005).

Jenny Ryan was the beauty who stole Robbie Ross's heart in 'In Camera' (2005) and had appeared previously as a scientist in 'New Life' (2003). She recently appeared in *Rebus*.

Chapter 7

Taggart is Dead, Long Live *Taggart*

After Mark McManus died, no one expected
Taggart to continue. How could it? Detective
Chief Inspector Jim Taggart was *Taggart*, wasn't
he? Executive producer Robert Love thought
differently, however, and was determined that
the team of actors who had surrounded McManus,
and who had grown so familiar to the television
audience for over eleven years, should be given
the chance to shine. The Taggart name, he was
convinced, could live on through them.

Taggart's young detective constable was new blood and new life.

'Mark McManus had said to me, in what turned out to be the last months of his life, that he'd hoped the show could carry on without him, with the young ones,' says Robert Love. 'For that reason, I felt it was the right thing for us to carry on. My first decision then was whether or not to replace the Taggart figure.

'I didn't want to recast the role of Jim Taggart because I felt that Mark's performance – the way he created that character – was unique. Anyone else coming in at that time would be forced either to having to reproduce Mark McManus or they would have taken it in another direction. I felt it would be stronger to build up the already established characters. And I think I was proven right.'

Robert's approach made a lot of sense. Mark's ill health had meant greater than expected exposure for Reid and Jardine in recent years anyway. However, ITV needed to be convinced that a detective series without its main detective could work.

'I had to persuade the network that Jardine and Reid – in other words, James and Blythe – could be the stars and that that would be a better formula for a continuing series than trying to bring someone in,' explains Robert.

'The other thing was the business of what to call it. Do you call it *Taggart* when Taggart is dead? I don't think there is another example like it, of the eponymous hero leaving and the show carrying on. People have recast characters, but that is a different thing.

'What I said to the network was that rather than simply being the name of a character, *Taggart* was in effect a brand name, which meant a detective whodunit set in Glasgow.'

A funeral and a murder

In STV and Robert Love's favour was *Taggart's* undeniable popularity – 'Violent Delights' had been watched by a peak audience of 18.3 million on 1 January 1992, and it regularly pulled in well over 12 million viewers. Another factor was that a three-parter and a two-hour special were already well into pre-production.

'Legends', by Barry Appleton, was a story of revenge and murder surrounding the reunion of a 1960s pop group, the Adders. Love had already planned that this episode would mark a change – the introduction of a new regular cast member.

Colin McCredie had appeared in two previous episodes of *Taggart*, most memorably as 'Sandy the fat farmhand' – as Colin himself describes the role – in the gothic maelstrom of 'Hellfire' (1994). Love had enjoyed this performance, and decided to introduce Colin as the new keen-as-mustard detective constable.

However, the script for 'Legends' didn't really allow the series to mark the passing of Jim Taggart. Instead, it was adapted, with many 'Mark scenes' rewritten to suit Colin. Meanwhile, Robert sat down with Glenn Chandler and together they devised a way of saying farewell to Jim in the two-hour standalone planned for broadcast that year.

As a result, 'Black Orchid' was the first post-McManus episode to be screened, in February 1995. Poignantly, it began with a wake for the dead DCI. 'We thought the audience would appreciate it – that it would offer a sense of closure, if you like,' Robert observes.

Of course, the *Taggart* team were well used to filming wakes over the years – so many corpses mean so many funerals – and the scenes here are moving. Then as Jardine returns to the office and looks through Jim's old desk, he reacts in characteristically prickly fashion when Julian Glover's stand-in superintendent – Iain Anders was missing due to ill health – asks where Jim Taggart is.

Jim Taggart's funeral was an emotional affair.

'We've just been at his funeral, sir,' comes the response.

However, it's then pretty much business as usual as the corpses and murder suspects mount up.

'After the first ten or fifteen minutes of "Black Orchid", Mark was only referred to about twice and that was quite deliberate,' Glenn Chandler points out. 'We were saying, "These are the guys you're watching now. It's going to be the same sort of show, but you've got some different characters here."'

Glenn and Robert's confidence *Taggart* could carry on hadn't been shared by everyone. Stuart Hepburn, who had starred in the early series as DS Kenny Forfar and had gone on to write several episodes, including 'Rogues' Gallery' (1990), had met with Murray Ferguson, the series producer on 'Legends', and warned that the audience wouldn't accept the programme without Jim Taggart in it. Recalling that ominous prediction today, he laughs, 'Shows you how much I knew.'

But the new leads in the show, though happy to get their chance, had doubts of their own. Duff recalls telling friends, 'I don't see how this can work,' while Macpherson remembers a particularly gloomy outlook: '"Double Bob" – Robert Robertson – hadn't long come back after his heart attack at that time, and Iain Anders had a heart attack, too, and had missed "Black Orchid",' says James. 'As a result, Blythe and I were starting to talk about the curse of *Taggart*. I thought it guaranteed us work for one episode, and then I thought yeah, that'd be it.'

'Good stories are always the key'

Having lost its star, *Taggart* had a lot to prove, so it had gone back to basics and concentrated on serving up terrific whodunit storylines.

'Good stories are always the key,' says James Macpherson. 'Get the story right and you know it will work. With Glenn, for instance, you knew when

the story came in that you'd think, "That's weird." In his scripts, strange things happened; it was never like any other show. Whether it was the occult or some sort of strange murder, you always said, "That's interesting." As for Robert, there's a saying, "Trust a man who knows." Well, Robert was that man. He knew.'

'These are the guys you're watching now.'

For Glenn, the absence of Mark McManus offered a new challenge. 'In a way, it was exciting to be able to explore other relationships,' he admits. 'We all missed Mark dearly, but we had to move on and we had some great fun with the stories we did after that. Some were very different.'

The first outing without McManus, 'Black Orchid', was exactly the cracking yarn the team needed, arguably one of Chandler's best. Robert Love had assembled an impressive cast, including James Laurenson, who'd played a *Taggart* murderer once before in 'Double Jeopardy' (1988), as crafty stage hypnotist the Great Sabina, and Amanda Redman as a femme fatale cabaret singer.

The deliciously convoluted plot was packed with equal measures of showbiz sleaze and flights of fancy – from feuding hypnotists to a murder on a sunbed – and even offered viewers their first experience of that loveable, irritating know-it-all detective constable, Stuart Fraser.

In the pre-credits sequence, Fraser takes part in the Great Sabina's stage show and is hypnotised. Embarrassing enough, you would think, to be hoodwinked into trying to arrest an entire theatre-full of people, but Fraser then agrees to be hypnotised a second time in order to prove Sabina could get a person to do things they didn't want to do. As a result, he confidently accuses his senior officer of being a rapist before being brought out of his

Duff's Jackie Reid in 'Dead Man's Chest': hard-working, independent and extremely watchable.

'trance'. Most cops would get the sack for such behaviour, but for Fraser and Colin McCredie it was the start of an association with the programme that continues to this day.

For ITV, it was ultimately down to the numbers, but on this account everyone was pleasantly surprised. 'When the ratings came back, there was simply no change,' recalls Robert. 'James and Blythe were now the leads, but we were still getting the same viewing figures of around twelve or thirteen million. The audience was still there.'

With the narrative focusing on two much younger detectives, the new *Taggart* was already breaking its own conventions. No longer would the face of Glasgow's police look like a battle-worn ex-boxer. Jardine and Reid, with their sculpted hair and cheekbones, might have passed as the lead singers of a Glasgow pop band.

'*Taggart* was never soapy,' Robert points out. 'We always felt that what made it strong was the story, that that was the driving force of it. After Mark died, we didn't have the kind of family background he'd had with Jean and the daughter who was always getting into trouble. That kind of intimate personal story was diminished. Jardine always had a girlfriend – it always went wrong – and Reid had boyfriends. But the whodunit was paramount.'

Times were changing, too. In the early 1980s it had made sense for Jim Taggart to be a working-class man, happy to eat his lunchtime pie in the pub his parents used to go to. In contrast, Jardine and Reid were typical of young professionals of a different decade. So when, in 'Angel Eyes' (1996), Jardine moves into a new flat, it is a smart conversion in a Victorian house, the kind of property any twenty-something would aspire to own. But beyond that we seldom learn anything of his home life.

As for Reid, she was clearly hard-working and independent, but there were only fleeting glimpses of a life or relatives beyond the office. She visits family in 'Dead Man's Chest' (1996), but the link here is essential to the plot.

'I never really thought what her back story was,' comments Glenn Chandler with a shrug. 'I never felt it was terribly important. I never consciously thought, "Where has she come from?" She was so good when she was there on screen I felt you never needed a background for her.'

Breaking new ground

Perhaps the most surprising development in the series in the mid-1990s was the outing of DC Stuart Fraser.

D'ye ken?

Blythe Duff and her husband, Tom Forrest, awoke one morning in May 2000 to find their home had been burgled as they'd slept. But when the crook read that it was the home the *Taggart* 'tec' shared with a real-life policeman, he contacted a newspaper and arranged for their goods to be returned.

> 'When the ratings came back, there was simply no change. James and Blythe were now the leads, but we were still getting the same viewing figures.'

DC Fraser in 'Angel
Eyes': young,
gifted and gay.

No one had ever dared to have a gay cop on a mainstream television show before, and for a series set on the mean streets of Glasgow, this hint of pink liberation seemed quite a departure.

In fact, there had been gay subplots and references in several episodes of *Taggart*, as far back as 'The Killing Philosophy' (1987), when one murder suspect is an army officer who turns out to be a gay man, and one lead takes Livingstone and Jardine 'undercover' in a gay club.

For Glenn Chandler, establishing Fraser's sexuality amidst a fast-paced plot involving a serial killer targeting Glasgow's fast-developing gay community was a victory for modern thinking. 'I don't think in the early days we'd have got away with "Angel Eyes" [1996],' the writer chuckles. 'It felt like a controversial thing to do. I remember I stuck out for the ending, which has both Reid and Fraser getting the hots for this one guy, and Fraser gets him. I was determined to get away with that – you couldn't have done it in any other detective series. Not at the time.'

Robert Love and Glenn Chandler had planned this development – revealed at the end of the first episode of 'Angel Eyes' – since introducing Colin McCredie as Fraser over a year before.

However, sensitive to the impact it would have if the audience were taken by surprise, they'd made the decision to keep it quiet. Indeed, even the actor in question was not told of their intentions.

D'ye ken?

Blythe teamed up with *Lord of the Rings* star Billy Boyd to launch the National Theatre of Scotland in February 2006. They starred in the show *Home*, performing in a high-rise block of flats in Glasgow's Easterhouse district, which was filmed by three men using hand-held cameras abseiling down the outside of the building. The pictures were beamed back live to a giant screen on the street below, watched by an audience of about a thousand people.

'In some ways, I think it wasn't a bad thing I didn't know,' Colin reflects. 'Others knew – costume people, directors – but not me. When I was told, it was a bit of a bombshell. I wasn't at all homophobic, but in an odd sort of way it felt like it was me who was coming out, not just Fraser. Also there was the newspaper reaction. One headline was something like "*Faggart*". And you get the odd "There's that poof out of *Taggart*" comment, but I take it in my stride,' Colin laughs. 'I usually tell people I'm more embarrassed playing a policeman than someone who is gay!

'I think he was the first gay main character on a British cop show. For a show like *Taggart* – which isn't about issues – it struck me as a very positive thing. I didn't play him any differently afterwards; I played him the same way I'd always done. He was a policeman who just happened to be gay – it's secondary to him doing his job.'

'Angel Eyes' was memorable for other reasons. 'We had some great funny moments,' says Glenn Chandler. 'It was a bit like when we needed the Hell's Angels for "Knife Edge" [1986], it was the kind of story where you couldn't just go to central casting for the right kind of people: you had to get the real thing. So we advertised and we got loads of gay people and a few drag queens to come out and we were filming in Dumbarton in an old club there. But the unit base was at the other end of the high street, so it meant everyone had to walk down through the town in the middle of the day. All these nightclubbers and drag queens walking down Dumbarton high street on a Monday afternoon, while all the old ladies were out doing the shopping – that was a laugh!'

Fraser and Jardine shared few lifestyle choices. The tension was palpable.

Unbutton it a bit, will you?

Taggart may not be issues-led drama, but it wouldn't be *Taggart* without some significant differences of opinion, and Fraser's sexuality was certainly not welcomed by all the characters. While Reid and even McVitie greeted the news with an open-minded shrug, Jardine had problems with it.

'Jardine had a very prissy attitude about gays,' says executive producer Robert Love. 'We had a lot of fun about Jardine's uptight approach.'

This was a symptom of a developing feature of Jardine's character: he wasn't someone who went out of his way to be likeable. Robert acknowledges he was 'quite complex for British television', but Glenn is rather more frank: 'To be honest, I wouldn't have liked to work with Jardine. He had a nice relationship with Reid, quite fraternal, but when Colin came along, they struck sparks off each other.'

'When I became the boss in the series, I thought, "Right, I'm going to have to row with people I used to be friends with,"' reflects James. 'You can't go to the pub and run with the guys any more – you have to be the boss and being the boss means "In you come, do that again and you are out."' Jardine became increasingly isolated from his peers. That he evolved as an oddly unsympathetic leading detective was down, at least in part, to James's interpretation of the role. 'I never ever went for the "I want you to love me" effect,' he reveals. 'That is what actors usually go for. But I thought, "I'm not going to do this," and so he was not a particularly likeable or loveable character; but the mail I get is weird because clearly some people do really like him. He was kind of homophobic – maybe homophobic is a bit strong, but his attitudes were of an old Scots Glaswegian.

'When Neil [Alastair] Duncan left, Jardine was something Taggart would immediately hate: a Christian and a non-drinker. But the great thing was that Taggart and Jardine got on,' continues James. 'After Mark died, Jardine became the cop with the problem. There was no one in his life, just a string of buggered-up relationships. Jardine was lonely, but never let it interfere with his job – you've got to work and do your job.'

Reid:	'Well?'
Jardine:	'Well what?'
Reid:	'Are congratulations in order?'
Jardine:	'No, they're not.'
Taggart:	'Turned you down, did she?'

'Gingerbread' (1993)

Opposite: After McManus died, Jardine became the cop with the problem.
Below: Jardine's attempts at a love life made for a long-running tragi-comic subplot. 'Angel Eyes', 1996.

Jardine: loser in love

Jardine's attempts to secure a girlfriend are a recurring tragi-comic subplot of *Taggart*. In 'Gingerbread' (1993), he falls for an old flame, Gemma Normanton, played by Fiona Gillies, a celebrated true-crime writer. Their affair moves forward with such speed he decides to propose marriage, only to find she already has a fiancé in London: she'd simply been using him for his police contacts. The fact all his police colleagues knew he was about to propose only made matters worse.

Other disastrous liaisons include, in 'Rogues' Gallery' (1990), the stunningly beautiful art dealer Valerie Sinclair, played by Edita Brychta, who seduces Jardine in her garden, but her involvement with a murdered business partner and status as a prime suspect put a dampener on things. And in 'Angel Eyes' (1996), Jardine gets close to the sister of one of the victims, only to discover that she is HIV positive. Later, in 'Football Crazy' (2000), he's tongue-tied and unable to ask a young WPC out on a date.

Fraser, Reid, Jardine and Ross were a new line-up for 'Football Crazy', 2000.

Robbie Ross: the dodgy DI

The addition of DI Robbie Ross to the *Taggart* team in 1997 (his first episode, 'A Few Bad Men', was screened in 1998) followed the death of Iain Anders and the on-screen promotion of Jardine to DCI. A junior detective was required alongside Reid and Fraser.

Jardine and Ross square up.

It was another unexpected piece of casting by executive producer Robert Love. Rather than bringing in an actor in place of the senior Anders in a like-for-like swap, he decided on a younger man, played by the rakish John Michie, to threaten Jardine's authority, and his position as Jackie Reid's closest confidante.

The change also coincided with

The *Taggart* boys jockey for position.

a new set for the police headquarters – a former cop shop in Govan, since vacated – giving the programme a rather different feel.

Immediately, the team were pitted against one another as whispers and rumours about the new man dogged the investigations into two apparently separate cases, which ended up being linked.

Michie was an instant hit with the majority of fans. They welcomed his 'lone gun' style, and the way he bent the rules, in stark contrast to Jardine's by-the-book approach.

'I thought it was great just to see what I could do with this character,' says John Michie. 'I wanted to really push the side of him that's irreverent, doesn't tow the line and that's flirty. I loved the fact he had a few criminal acquaintances in the past but that underneath it all his private life is a complete mess: he's separated, there's one child he never sees, and he still thinks he's a bit of a lad even though he's getting on. He's a flawed character. But he's confident in his work, that's what keeps him going. He can strut about, flash the badge and be the Robbie Ross that he thinks he is.'

Ross makes an entrance in 'A Few Bad Men'. ('He's not bad-looking,' Jackie Reid can't help but notice.)

From the beginning, however, Ross's inflated sense of self is regularly punctured by Fraser's wit. Theirs is an entertaining love-hate relationship. Fraser likes nothing better than to kid Ross about fancying him – a joke that was particularly clear in their early appearances together, when Ross was only just catching on that Fraser was gay.

'Ross is constantly taking the piss out of Fraser for being gay, but really they like each other,' says John Michie. 'Also, Ross would be lost without Fraser. He's not good on the computer, he just says, "Stuart, sort it out for me," and he does. Fraser saves him all the time.'

DI Robbie Ross is constantly dodging between the right and wrong sides of the law – and the right and wrong kinds of women. In 'A Few Bad Men' (1998), he is introduced as just back from suspension after accepting a holiday from a known criminal – though at the same time, Jackie Reid can't help but notice 'He's not bad-looking and he's got a sense of humour.'

In 'Fearful Lightning' (1999), his flirtation with Reid moves up a gear or two. First, he puts a rival off asking her out, then he invites her over for dinner himself. Jackie gets scrubbed up and buys a bottle of champagne in anticipation of a memorable night, only to find that he already has a woman in situ, *without* her clothes. In the following mystery, 'A Fistful of Chips' (1999), he's accepting stolen goods from a long-time 'contact', Jakey Miller, only for Jakey to end up dead. Not that that stops him from hitting on Jakey's girlfriend.

Ross is also put under investigation in 'Skin Deep' (2000) for accepting a £5,000 fine. But he is being framed and when Ross discovers the culprit, a petty criminal called Dougie Todd (played by former Marillion singer, Fish), he takes matters into his own hands by paying him a visit for what is a memorable fight scene.

Character versus plot

Robert Love retired from STV – by now part of a larger media company, the Scottish Media Group (SMG) – and from his position as *Taggart's* executive

Michie and Fish go head-to-head in 2000's 'Skin Deep'.

'Wavelength', 2000. The Reid-Holmes affair took *Taggart* away from the simple whodunit.

producer in 1999. What followed was a period of some instability for the programme and a change of direction that proved controversial.

Under the guidance of SMG's new head of drama, Philip Hinchcliffe, *Taggart* began to focus more on the regular characters and less on the whodunit storylines. The soap-opera element that Robert had so long argued against started to feature.

Ross and Reid get up close and personal in 'Falling in Love'.

This harked back to early days, but instead of Jim and Jean round the fire having a moan at each other, it was DI Ross and DS Reid flirting in a wine bar. For several episodes a complicated love story is played out to the usual background of 'deid' bodies, gunshot wounds and conspiracies. Then, in 'Wavelength' (2000), Reid announces she is getting engaged to DCI Brian Holmes from the Complaints and Discipline

department and Ross is shell-shocked by the news. Reid marries Holmes in 'Falling in Love' (2001), but the body language between the couple is never convincing and the audience is left in no doubt that Jackie is torn between Brian, Robbie and Michael.

For many fans, all this love intrigue was fascinating. For others, it detracted from the point of the show – the whodunit storylines.

Ratings war

The show needed to fight for its ratings and, in a competitive ITV world, needed to be more successful. Some aspects of the way *Taggart* developed in the late 1990s were successful, but others were not.

'When new characters come in, it not only changes the way you act with them, but it changes the amount of scenes and lines you have, and often you have to wait until that settles down a bit before you know where you are,' observes Blythe Duff. 'But bringing in Robbie Ross was a good thing because it made the dynamic between the characters quite different and I think it did work as a love triangle.

'Jardine and Ross were similar ages; it was interesting to ask whether there was any jealousy going on between them. With Jardine, Ross always felt he could duck and dive and get away with things. It showed the kind of arrogance he has – he often feels he knows better than other people.'

But it wasn't making everyone happy. James Macpherson, who had been with the programme for fifteen years, had some serious doubts. 'I don't know if the triangle was ever a great success,' he comments. 'Robbie Ross was the guy who'd go for the good-looking girls – he was the eye candy for women – but I felt *Taggart* wasn't about us, the characters. It was about good plots. Overall, I thought the show was sliding. It had a loss of humour.'

This feeling would soon lead to a dramatic death. But this time it wouldn't be Jardine investigating. He would be the victim.

Chapter 8

The Murder Business: Glasgow's Police

How does the *Taggart* team compare with the men and women who really police Glasgow? Someone who knows just how close to the truth the programme gets is former detective chief inspector Nanette Pollock, who is employed as an adviser.

'I tell you what they do brilliantly,' she says. 'To me, there is nothing entertaining about a murder. Interesting, yes, but not entertaining. But what *Taggart* manages to do is take the drama out of the murder and put that into the plot. That's what makes it work.'

'Have you seen this man?' Reid goes about her business in 'A Death Foretold'.

As adviser to *Taggart*, Nanette Pollock keeps the scriptwriters right about legal and police procedure, but she never forgets that at its heart the series is a whodunit, not a documentary.

On Nanette Pollock's mantelpiece is a framed, slightly faded colour photograph showing four rows of men and just two women. It's a picture of all the senior officers in Glasgow CID, but it's not ancient history: it dates from 2002. 'Of the two women in that picture, one's me and the other is the secretary,' she affirms. 'There are more women now, it's getting better, but back then I was the only one.'

Nanette started out her working life as a hairdresser's assistant, before shocking her parents by joining City of Glasgow Police in the 1970s. She won an early transfer to work as a plain-clothes detective in the male-dominated world of A Division CID, in Glasgow city centre. Over the next three decades Nanette rose through the ranks to detective chief inspector, the same rank as Alex Norton's character.

Pollock is Matt Burke crossed with Jackie Reid. Just as Blythe Duff's character was 'seconded' to work under Jim Taggart in 'Rogues' Gallery' (1990), so Nanette had to walk into a similar smoke-filled incident room in 1973.

'If I hadn't been twenty-seven, but nineteen or twenty, I wouldn't have been able to handle it,' she says, 'but because I was a wee bit more mature, I just listened and took it all in. It was really an eye-opener, all these detectives who'd been in CID for years and done murder after murder.

'When I got married to another detective, the rule then was you couldn't work together in the same office, so I got shipped out to the East End of the city – not him, me – and that was another learning experience. Having been in the city centre CID, I'd mainly had white-collar crime to deal with: a lot of businesses, plus violence, stabbings, shootings at the weekend. On my first day in the East End I got an incest case and I thought, "Is that what they do here?" Then the boss said, "I want you to work in Shettleston. They don't have a female up there." The first two cases there were incest, too. It wasn't all they did, but because I was the woman detective, I was dealing with family cases a lot, and it just seemed like it.'

Like Reid, Nanette worked hard, but unlike Reid, who has been stuck as a DS since the days Jim Taggart used to nibble Rich Tea biscuits, she regularly won promotion – her seniors recognising her talent. She worked all across the city, including an extended stint with the Drugs Squad as a detective inspector. Then, in 1997, she was made a DCI and shifted back into the city centre.

'I remember thinking, "Please, God, give me anything other than a prostitute murder or a disco murder,"' she says. 'But of course that's exactly what happened: two murders in the first few days.'

James Macpherson finds some unlikely inspiration for Jardine's character.

Glasgow has seen a series of prostitute murders since the 1980s. 'There was no serial killer,' Nanette says, 'just a series of men killing prostitutes.' But it was one particularly brutal slaying of a woman she had known well for several years that convinced Nanette she had to change the way the police approached the whole business of red-light areas.

'That was Margo Lafferty,' Nanette recalls with a shudder. 'She was found in a disused pen, a yard, at the back of a premises in West Regent Street Lane.' In the heart of the city centre's business district, this was nevertheless a favourite haunt of Glasgow's prostitute community.

'There was a large gate that led into the pen. She was found by some guy who'd come out from one of the pubs, having a cigarette on his break. He saw the gate flapping in the wind and went over to take a look and saw what he thought was a naked mannequin. But it was Margo, and her clothes had been stripped off.'

Nanette is now sixty-one and lives in a bungalow in a smart suburb of Glasgow. It is hard to imagine her taking a call in the middle of the night and being told, 'There's been a murder.' But Nanette was among the first at the scene of the crime.

'The sergeant had phoned and said they thought the victim was Margo,' she recalls. 'I knew her well, probably for about ten years, from visiting the drop-in centre. I knew she was a lesbian and that her lover was in jail at the time for carrying out a pretty horrific assault. I knew Margo was back on the game. But Margo was tough. I couldn't imagine anyone getting the better of her, so I remember saying if it is her, she'll have left a mark on the killer. She'd have fought back.'

The investigation that followed highlights the differences and similarities between real police work and what is depicted in *Taggart*. The major difference is one of scale.

'In *Taggart*, Burke's team are a little like a rural force; they have to do everything themselves. You don't see them calling on the kind of resources we have at our disposal,' explains Nanette.

'Of course, they are limited that way because they are a TV drama. But I could call on something like seventy-five officers, and we had the forensics back-up, and other teams we could bring in, too, if need be.'

Finding Margo Lafferty's killer had less to do with detectives' hunches or inspired deduction than it did with a systematic approach.

Burke leads the investigation from the whiteboard in 2005's 'Cause to Kill'.

'We had a lot of leads called in,' she says. 'There was a lot of media interest because it was a prostitute murder, and SMG were just across from my office at the time, so we used the television as much as we could to keep the issue in people's minds.

'Someone rang in, and said, "You should check out this guy I know: his face was a mess the day after the murder."'

The killer was Brian Donnelly and he'd been out drinking to celebrate his nineteenth birthday. The next day he'd gone with mates to watch a football match, explaining the bruises and cuts on his face away with a story about getting into a fight at a taxi queue.

'He thought he'd finish his night out with a prostitute, as some men do,' scowls Nanette. 'Only, whatever happened, he ended up killing her.

'But the lead simply went on to the pile; he was someone to be checked out in turn. It was only when the detectives got to him that it clicked, "Yes, he could be the one."'

Donnelly was successfully tried and convicted of the murder; a speck of his blood too small for the eye to see was found on Margo's underclothes.

'Prostitutes never remove their clothing. The only way for that blood to be there was if he'd killed her,' Nanette says. 'It was a DNA match.'

The appliance of science

The *Taggart* team get gloved up and ready for forensic action in 'A Death Foretold'.

Ian Hamilton is the head of the biology branch of the Forensic Support department of Strathclyde Police. In the last twenty-five years he has seen a massive change in the scientific nature of murder investigations, mainly through the introduction of DNA testing. But he warns that while the science has proven a boom, it has its limitations.

One particularly ugly murder case in Glasgow went to underline the power of DNA testing. Farah Noor Adams, who lived in the city's West End, had just dropped her daughter off at school and decided to go on a power walk along the Kelvin Walkway. It was the middle of a Friday morning, but she was attacked, raped and murdered in a seemingly senseless crime. Her body was left only a short distance from where they found the first victim in *Killer* (1983). The public was outraged: an attractive thirty-nine-year-old single mum robbed of life.

It later emerged that she attempted to call 999 on her mobile while being followed, but due to some quirk with her phone service, her plea for help wasn't put through.

Ian Hamilton's forensic scientists got to work at the murder scene straight away. By the Monday, just as detectives were about to walk into a press conference to appeal for the public's help in finding the killer, they had a result: a DNA sample taken from the victim's body matched that of a Thomas Waddell, a nineteen-year-old who lived in nearby Maryhill.

'I've often said you need to commit two crimes to be caught by DNA. The first crime is when they take your sample; the second one is when they match you from the database,' says Hamilton.

However, such magical results do not happen if the perpetrator is not one of the 2.5 million or so people on the national DNA database.

'I think some detectives see forensics as a holy grail. It's not there to replace police work, simply to aid it,' says Hamilton. 'The police officers are thinking from the start, "What forensics opportunities do we have here?"'

Reid enters the cordoned-off crime scene.

In that sense, forensics leads the investigation. But there are limits. We can't usually take DNA from the breath on a wall, for instance. We need to know where to look. And if someone isn't on the database, other detective procedures have to take over.'

Hamilton heads a department of some thirty-eight scientists. In *Taggart* in recent years there have been two forensic specialists, Gemma Kerr (Lesley Harcourt) and Sheila Crombie (Tamara Kennedy).

'Our staff are often young women, so *Taggart* has been quite accurate there,' says Hamilton. 'We are seeing more and more female graduates wanting to come into this line of work and quite often they are simply better than their male contemporaries.'

Naw, you cannae do that...

Willie Johnstone was a detective superintendent – the rank above Burke – with Strathclyde Police until 2006, when he left to work for a private firm providing analysis of phone calls for evidence in criminal cases.

An investigation is not all about hunches. There's plenty of theory and paperwork, too.

'Across Scotland the detective supers get the more serious cases to be in charge of,' says Johnstone. 'If it is a domestic murder, then the super wouldn't

John Michie got more than he bargained for when he went along to Hamilton CID to meet some real-life Robbie Rosses.

'I wanted to do some research into being a DI in Glasgow and went along to speak to them in their office. While I was there, I could hear on this intercom thing that an interrogation was going on in the next room.

'Well, the interrogation was getting more and more violent all the time. I was hearing it all come through the loudspeaker, but all the cops were standing about laughing and drinking coffee. I could hear a slap and a hit – I was getting more and more upset – then someone saying, "Oh, you effing bastard you."

'I was there with Tom Forrest, Blythe's husband, and I turned to him and said, "What's going on? Should I be hearing this?"

'The others, Tom included, were like, "It's no problem. Do you want to go see what's happening?" My loyalties were really split: I felt I should probably report a case of police brutality, but Tom had invited me into this office, so I went through and I saw this ned being interviewed by a cop. The ned started swearing at me – "Who the F are you?" – and this cop told me to say my name for the interview tape. My voice was shaking when I said, "John Michie." I thought I could see the bruises and blood where the cop had hit this guy, and then they said for the purposes of the tape everyone else had to say their names. It got round to the ned, and he starts smiling and says he was Detective Sergeant whatever it was. And suddenly they were all howling with laughter, this guy was some undercover specialist and he'd totally fooled me. He was quite an actor.

'Later we went for a drink in the pub next door and suddenly there's a girl outside threatening to throw herself off a roof. I said to the guys, "You can't fool me again," but this time it was a real-life incident. The poor lassie was OK, though; they got her down all right.'

Even Robbie Ross would disapprove of some of the things CID get up to.

be involved. But if it is the murder of a child, or a political figure, a police officer, a politician, someone the media would be interested in, or if there were any racist elements to it, then the detective super would get it.

'Detective work is now much more formalised than it was twenty-five years ago. In the past, detectives picked up their methods as they went along. Nowadays there is a book – it's that thick.' He holds up his fist. 'It's called the *Homicide Investigation Manual* – or the *Murder Manual* – and it's produced by the National Centre for Policing Excellence, also called Centrex.'

The *Murder Manual* was compiled to answer concerns that detective investigations success rates could vary between different forces. Relying on a hunch is one thing if you are Robbie Ross, but not if you are a real-life cop.

'They gathered together the senior detective experience in the country – including Scotland – and they wrote the *Homicide Investigation Manual*,' Willie says. 'It lays guidelines by which investigators will be judged. In other words, if things go wrong, here's the Bible, this is what you should be doing.

'Now I've never heard any of these things referred to in *Taggart*, but there isn't a major murder inquiry in the UK where Centrex is not involved in some way – either notionally in the background or as a physical presence.

'In the early days murders were solved by a team of detectives, but now you've got this manual and if a murder is unsolved after twenty-eight days, it is reviewed by another senior investigating officer. It's not about criticism, it's about supporting that investigation: we've reviewed that, we want to extend the house to house, do something else in the media. It is very scientific.

'I was always happy to have my investigations reviewed because no one is always right all the time. The bottom line is it's to ensure nothing is missed at an early enough stage to make a difference. A year down the line is often too late, often by then you've missed the boat.'

D'ye ken?

Willie Johnstone used to be based at the former Govan nick *Taggart* took over to use as its own cop shop in the late 1990s. 'It was always funny to watch the programme and to see Robbie Ross sitting at my old desk,' he laughs.

...And you can't do that, either!

- In *Taggart*, Mike Jardine received two major promotions – from DS to DI and to DCI – without ever leaving the one office. Similarly, Jackie Reid has stayed with the same unit for seventeen years and Fraser for twelve. But in real life, cops tend to move about; to get promotion, they go to different divisions.
- Before becoming a DCI, Nanette Pollock had to spend a year in uniform and work in the Complaints and Discipline division, as DCI Brian Holmes did. These mundane realities aren't reflected much by *Taggart*.

- A cop of Alex Norton's rank would seldom leave the office. He'd be too busy collating information from behind his desk and managing a team of officers that would count in the dozens. And as for visiting the crime scene, in the last few years even that has changed.

- Willie Johnstone underlines how thorough police work needs to be at every stage of an investigation. He gives one example: a relatively routine murder in a busy pub. However he recalls 'about fifty' witness statements claiming they'd been in the toilet at the time it happened and didn't see anything. 'We worked out the square footage of the toilet and we knew all those people couldn't have been in there,' he says. 'It sounds flippant, but when you are going to court, you need to be sure of all the facts. We knew some people were lying, because it wasn't physically possible.'

- A common theme in *Taggart* is the sense of urgency when a body is found. Blythe Duff knows from her husband, a former detective sergeant, that when there's a murder it's 'all hands to the pump'. 'We talk of a golden twenty-four-hour period,' confirms Willie Johnstone.

In reality, DCI Burke wouldn't have time for hand-to-hand combat with criminals. 'The Ties That Bind', 2005.

'History dictates that what you do in that first day has a good effect in terms of the gathering of evidence. That is your opportunity – you have to grasp it. You have to get to witnesses straight away, before they have a chance to collude. That's why there is an urgency if there is a murder. If we have reasonable grounds to suspect you have committed a murder, the urgency provisions of the law allow us to come into your house without a warrant. But fourteen days down the line, we'd need a warrant, and by then the evidence might not be there.'

■ Not everything is done at break-neck speed. Something that *Taggart* has hinted at since 2001 is the importance now being put on forensics in detective work. This has affected everything to do with a murder scene. You no longer see any real-life Jim Taggart breezing his way up to a body and rifling through the victim's pockets to find a wallet. 'If, for example, we suspect a body has been buried, say in a wood, we might get an expert – a botanist, perhaps – who can come and tell us if they

'Not everything is done at break-neck speed.' Fraser and Reid decide not to rush into things. 'Bad Blood', 2003.

Ross gets personal. 'Dead Man Walking', 2005.

think the ground has been disturbed. I once got someone to explain what molehills looked like, to identify patches of disturbed ground to say whether it could have been done by moles. I was covering all the angles,' says Willie. 'In *Taggart*, those experts often just arrive at the scene; it's a drama and they don't have the time to do it otherwise, but in my job I've stopped experts going on to a scene, stopped pathologists going on to a scene. As the senior officer, it's up to me to decide who gets access and when. I'd often do that from my office. I'd rather get the forensic scientist in recovering hair, blood, DNA before anyone else goes in. That's why we immediately appoint a crime-scene manager – usually a DS – who coordinates the approach to the scene. It's not haphazard; it's very scientific and based on the information you have at the time.'

D'ye ken?

Your DNA is, generally speaking, unique to you, but the odds are lower on your having the same DNA as a fellow family member, and identical twins *do* have the same DNA. 'Identical twins have come up in a case,' says Ian Hamilton of Strathclyde Police Forensic Support. 'There was a rape where one identical twin said it wasn't him but his brother. However, the brother had an alibi and he didn't.'

■ While the *Taggart* detectives often 'get personal' on a case, Willie Johnstone warns that a good policeman always insulates himself from the results his hard work on a murder inquiry might garner. 'I never took cases personally,' he says. 'I've seen some good officers chewed up because the court result hasn't been what it should have been. We are human beings, but you have to stand back; it's not our role to get involved that way. As long as we can walk away and say, "We've done everything possible," then that's enough.'

Chapter 9

Taggart in the 21st Century

By 2000 ITV were putting pressure on SMG to improve *Taggart*'s ratings performance. Stuart Hepburn, a regular member of the *Taggart* cast in the 1980s who had turned television writer, got a call from his agent. The *Taggart* people wanted to talk to him. The meeting, which took place at SMG's London offices, was in effect a council of war. 'Numbers are down, it's going to get cut,' they told Hepburn. 'What do you think is wrong with it?'

Opposite: Norton's DCI Burke – 'a tough Scottie dug in the middle of it all' – arrived in 2002.

'I said something along the lines of, "The same thing that was wrong with it seven years ago. Mark McManus isn't in it,"' the writer recalls. 'And they asked me what I thought it needed to keep going. And I said, "Reinvent Mark McManus. You have to create a tough Scottie dug in the middle of it all who's going to stand there with a leg at each corner and tell you what the truth is, so get a major Scottish actor and reinvent it back to what it used to be."'

Stuart went home and wrote a treatment for a relaunch of the show featuring this tough 'Scottie dug', DCI Matt Burke, delivering it just three weeks later. However, for Stuart, that meeting about *Taggart* was just that: a meeting. It was an opportunity to throw some ideas around and speak his mind. He knew – as with many such meetings in television – there was little chance of his blueprint being taken up, especially as his proposal left no room for Detective Chief Inspector Mike Jardine.

'The consequences of what I was saying were very serious for James's character, and James was the lead,' he explains. 'If he'd looked at the treatment and said, "Under no circumstances," then it probably wouldn't have happened.'

But in fact no such obstacle existed. It wasn't yet announced to the public, but James had already decided to leave the show after a remarkable fifteen-year run.

'*Taggart* was only ever commissioned a year or a series at a time, so although it was fifteen years of my life, it wasn't like I'd taken the role expecting to be there that long,' comments Macpherson. 'I'd not been happy in *Taggart* because of changes at the top.'

Then came the crucial factor: on a flight from Glasgow to London in 2000, James suffered a collapsed lung. The condition, pneumothorax, required two emergency operations. Because he received medical attention quickly, his life wasn't seriously threatened – indeed, he was more concerned about his football team, Rangers, playing in the Champions League. But it was a timely wake-up call. With the fate of his late co-star, Mark McManus, also in his mind, he decided to make a change.

'I got ill and I realised I wanted to do other things,' says James. 'Things were also changing within the programme, so it was a bit of all those things together. They gave me the option of a death and I thought I'd go for that because I don't want to go back. I've watched soaps where people return after a while and it is usually a mistake.'

Eric Coulter, SMG's new head of drama, was the man now in charge of the show. Eric in turn introduced Graeme Gordon as the series producer, and together they realised they had a terrific opportunity open to them. They could reinvent *Taggart*, the most successful television show ever made in Scotland.

'They gave me the option of a death and I thought I'd go for that because I don't want to go back.'

With no expense spared on special effects, Jardine feels the heat.

Anything was possible

'Axing the show was never seriously considered as a possibility,' says Eric Coulter. 'In this day and age if a show is working, if it has a brand, if it gets the figures, you'd be mad to get rid of it. And from our point of view, if SMG axed *Taggart*, there is no guarantee that ITV would give us another show to replace it.

'So although when Mark McManus died, there were discussions at that point as to whether the show could continue or not, when I joined, it was actually a question of "How can we make the show continue?" What we were doing was getting it back on course.'

'I really hadn't watched the recent episodes of *Taggart* that much,' admits Graeme Gordon. 'But when I got the job, I then watched several of the recent ones to see what our starting point was. We asked ourselves, "What do we feel is working? And what can be changed? Is it a good recipe that just needs spicing up, or what?"'

For the existing cast, the approach was a welcome one. 'We'd changed producer every year for three or four years,' recalls Colin McCredie. '*Taggart* is very much based in Glasgow, and Eric and Graeme provide a very steady ship, plus they are based here. They had to get to know the show, but they are working-class guys with their feet very much on the ground and they know the job. They brought realism and gravitas to the show. It was a challenge to them, but that meant they wanted to make it work.'

Coulter and Gordon decided a fresh approach was needed if the *Taggart* brand was to be revived. Robert Robertson – the last surviving cast member from the original pilot, *Killer* – had just passed away, and it seemed the right moment to take a different approach. Stuart Hepburn's proposed treatment struck a chord with both of them, but they realised more was at stake than simply choosing a different kind of lead detective to replace Jardine.

'I thought what we had in *Taggart* at that time was a family, but there wasn't any head of the family,' observes Eric. 'We just had a lot of siblings. In the new shows, Burke is clearly the head of the family. So I never saw it as about replacing Mark McManus as such, but about putting in a strong authority figure.

'We felt all of our characters were working. Obviously Jackie Reid, Blythe, is very strong and many people identify with her. Then there is Robbie, slightly wide boy, the wayward one, and Fraser, the sort of geeky one, the wee brother.

'What didn't seem to be working was the someone above them who was very much the boss. Jardine was too similar in age to the others.'

'It didn't feel right to us that James Macpherson was trying to tell this cool guy, Robbie Ross, how to behave,' adds Graeme. 'You needed someone with just a bit more power than that. I felt that, and a lot of other people did, too. James leaving was an opportunity to reinvent that.'

Part of *Taggart*'s charm has always been the fact it is set in Glasgow – the accents, the landscape and many

D'ye ken?

One of the images used in the title sequence for the 2002 series was an exploding building from 'Fire, Burn'. If you look carefully, you can see Fraser running from the blast with a big grin on his face. 'The explosion was much bigger than any of us was expecting,' Colin McCredie explains, 'so when I turn away, I burst into a fit of nervous giggles.'

of the storylines are impossible to imagine anywhere else. The new production team felt this sense of place should be paramount. 'We wanted an actor who brought his own gravitas but also someone rooted to the city,' says Graeme. 'We watched a few of the episodes and thought they could have been set anywhere.'

Something else the team wanted to avoid in future was a creeping sense that *Taggart*'s classic whodunit format was being submerged in soap. The show was still to have strong characters, but Eric and Graeme were determined – as Robert Love had been before them – that they should not be distracted too much from the job of detecting a murder. The romantic subplots that had weaved through previous shows would not be repeated. The focus would be on the whodunit.

Burke makes his first dramatic appearance in 'Death Trap', January 2002.

Reinvention

Television had changed since the early 1980s: plots were now expected to be told at a faster pace, and the kind of three-parters that Glenn Chandler had excelled at – with their various red herrings and cliffhangers – were largely a thing of the past. With the new production regime in place at SMG's offices, Glenn Chandler decided it was time to take a step back from writing on the show. It was therefore up to Stuart to reinvent the series for a new age. Enter the mysterious figure of DCI Matt Burke, with an agenda all his own.

'I wanted Burke to have no family encumbrances because families are a nightmare in police stories,' Stuart says. 'Look what happened to Blythe's character – Reid got engaged and was married off. Why do that? It is better to just have her and Robbie Ross as lovelorn solos. With Burke, we just decided there were problems with his father, who is still around. He'd had a wife, has children, end of story. He lives alone and is dedicated to the job. That's all you need.'

The essentials of Burke's character decided, the issue now was who should play him. A clear front runner for the role existed, and it wasn't Alex Norton.

Prior to Coulter's arrival, contact had been made between SMG and the veteran actor Maurice Roëves, who'd starred in the award-winning 1980s BBC series *Tutti Frutti* alongside Emma Thompson and Robbie Coltrane, and the press considered him a shoo-in. However, negotiations did not go well.

'That's when we went to Alex,' says Coulter.

'Oh, no! It'll be as the pathologist'

'I had a feeling it would work out – that I would bring something of value to the part,' says Alex Norton.

With twenty-twenty hindsight, Alex Norton was an obvious contender for the top job at Glasgow CID. He'd memorably played a guest role in the third *Taggart* series, 'Knife Edge' (1986), as a butcher disposing of body parts around the city, and few long-serving fans of the show don't retain the image of him in a white coat stirring a bucket of blood to make black pudding. But since then he'd enjoyed a varied film and television career, as well as written for and performed on stage. Indeed, to some, it seemed unlikely that he'd want to be tied down by a series.

'My brother rang me up,' recalls Norton. '"I see you are in the papers," he said. "The headline is 'Who Will Be the New Taggart?'" I was like, "Oh, aye?" I told him you didn't believe anything in the papers.

'I didn't know anything about it. I put the phone down and thought, "Wonder if there is any truth in that?" And then I thought, "That would be good." But I had to put it in the back of my mind. Pretend I'd never heard it.

'Then I came up to Glasgow to film a pilot for a BBC series that never happened called *The Fabulous Bagel Boys*. When I arrived, my driver, who drives all the stars who come to Scotland and knows everything that is going on, said to me, "Ah, Mr Norton, terrible you were that close to getting *Taggart*. But you didn't get it. It's gone to Maurice Roëves."

'And I thought, "I wish I hadn't heard that." It put a dampener on the whole trip, was in my heid the whole time during the thing I was working on. But nobody had called me or auditioned me, or anything.

'Next thing my agent called and asked if I'd meet Graeme Gordon and Eric Coulter about going into *Taggart*. And I thought, "Oh, no, it'll be as the pathologist. And do I really want to be the pathologist, with all that expository dialogue?" 'Ah, yes, it was a two-and-a-half-inch wound; it penetrated the lower left vertebrae.'" That's a tough job, so I said, "No, I don't think I want to be the pathologist." Then the agent said, "No, it's the senior detective." But I was like, "No, no, my driver told me I wasn't getting that..."

'Anyway, I went to meet them in Soho and they told me negotiations had been broken off with Maurice and do I want to do it? And I said words to the effect of "Yes, I do."'

The role was immediately appealing. 'I thought I would be right for it. I thought I had the weight behind me, the age I am at. If they'd asked me ten years before, maybe I wouldn't have been able to do it. I'd have been too lightweight. I thought, "This is the right job for me at the right time to do it." Deep within, I had a feeling it would work out – that I would bring something of value to the part.

'So I was just delighted. But you never want to say anything until your name is on the contract, and even then you are cautious. I kept it schtum until the contract came in and I signed it. That was the day I jumped up and down in the kitchen and had champagne and lobster with the wife.'

For Eric Coulter and Graeme Gordon, there was no doubt Norton was the actor they most wanted in the role of Burke. At the age of fifty, he was a similar age to Mark McManus when he took the role of Jim Taggart in 1983. And Graeme had worked with him before on the film *Beautiful Creatures*, which starred Rachel Weisz. 'I was playing a particularly nasty detective in it,' recalls Alex. 'It was a good film and a great part because it gets darker and darker as it goes along and this guy gets more and more unpleasant. In a way, I think of that as my audition for *Taggart*.'

But there was no guarantee ITV would approve of him. As far as the network's director of drama in London, Nick Elliot, was concerned, *Taggart* was a series in need of a leading man. Was Alex Norton an ITV leading man?

Graeme explains, 'We made up a show reel to take to the network. Nick Elliot was worried he wasn't sexy enough, wasn't handsome

D'ye ken?

What makes the perfect *Taggart*? 'Firstly, a good whodunit,' says Eric Coulter. 'You have to have multiple suspects. They all have to be in the story, the killer has to be in the story, the audience has to have enough clues so that when you reveal the killer, you realise the clues were there and that you haven't picked up on them. And you need to give a really good emotional investment for our regular characters.'

'I thought I had the weight behind me, the age I am at. If they'd asked me ten years before, maybe I wouldn't have been able to do it.'

enough. But we gave him examples, actors like Michael Gambon and David Jason, who are big stars in Britain but you wouldn't say they are physically attractive.'

'We did have to sell Alex to the network,' Eric confirms. 'But we were pushing against an opening door. So although he wasn't a big ITV name when we gave them examples of Alex's work, Nick Elliot said, "Fine." But it was on our heads if it didn't work out!'

'Death Trap'

Stuart Hepburn, who was given the responsibility of writing the new episode, found himself teasing out the plot amidst conflicting emotions. He and James Macpherson were old friends from their time working on the show together as actors. Now he was going to have to kill him off.

'Death Trap', broadcast in January 2002, is a gloriously involved two-

hour story at the start of which the son of a Glasgow councillor is killed by a high-velocity rifle through the window of his own flat. The death appears to be linked to a contentious property development, and when personal animosity between the grieving councillor and Jardine starts getting in the way of the investigation, Mike finds himself removed from the case.

It's a clever piece of plotting: events in Glasgow's fictional CID reflecting the new direction in production. Jardine's isolation parallels Macpherson's own imminent departure from the show. Burke seems to be plotting to get rid of Jardine – just as Norton's arrival marks the ousting of Macpherson.

When Jardine doggedly continues the investigation on his own, he is lured

into meeting a contact next to the Clyde. Surprised from behind, he is thrown into the river and drowns, his body swept miles out into the estuary. It is found the next day on mudflats at Langbank.

'We had to do several takes of that scene of us discovering Jardine's body, and each time the tears were real,' Blythe Duff recalls.

The episode ends with Jardine's poignant funeral, during which Blythe gives the eulogy – a wonderfully poised performance guaranteed to leave no eye dry.

Taggart: back from the dead

Eric Coulter had recruited director Ian Madden, an experienced hand on television and film, to create a new *Taggart* look.

'*Taggart* had got away from its urban nature, and its grittiness, so we brought it back to the city,' Madden says. 'In "Death Trap", I shot the whole thing in the city centre and on the streets. There were situations where you had to just buy what you got and hope the general public wouldn't get in the way too much.'

Indeed, Glasgow had seldom looked better. From the twilight of run-down Garnethill to dawn on the mudflats, to the decaying industrial setting of the docks, 'Death Trap' is a visually striking television movie that served to set the new standard.

'We want these films to feel like an event,' explains Eric Coulter. 'It's not just another episode of *The Bill*. With *Taggart*, you want to feel you are sitting down and watching a film, with those production values.'

When they finished filming, everyone knew it was the end of an era, as well as the start of a new one.

In terms of filming, James's final *Taggart* scene wasn't the moment he was killed – that was done earlier in the production process. Rather, it was

'We want these films to feel like an event,' explains producer Eric Coulter. Behind the scenes for 'The Thirteenth Step'.

DCI Burke – a modern Jim Taggart.

the scene in which he bursts into a senior commander's office to complain about the way the investigation is being handled, only to find Matt Burke is already there, waiting to replace him.

'"Death Trap" is still one of my absolute favourites,' says Blythe Duff. 'What Reid goes through on screen mourning the loss of Mike Jardine was mirroring how I felt saying goodbye to James.'

'It was very moving,' agrees John Michie. 'I thought one of the best shots ever in *Taggart* was the long shots of the mudflats – it was beautifully done. Ally Walker was the director of photography and Ian Madden was directing, and they did it really well. And Blythe was great in the emotional scenes.'

'James leaving was a great excuse for a great story,' adds Colin McCredie. 'It was a great episode to be involved in because although we were sad James was going, it was also exciting that Alex was coming in.'

Burke: the new boss

DCI Matt Burke didn't just arrive at the offices of Glasgow CID; he exploded. Like a homemade incendiary taped to the bottom of a gangster's car boot, he changed those around him for ever.

Alex Norton might have been born to play the role of the tough, hard-working cop. As Mark McManus had done almost twenty years previously,

Alex's arrival on the *Taggart* set represented a prodigal's return to Glasgow after years away working in London. And like Jim Taggart, Burke isn't out to take any prisoners. In that first, memorable episode, 'Death Trap', he goes head to head with the man he has to replace, Mike Jardine, and it is an encounter no one could forget. Neither man was giving an inch.

'The thing about Burke, for me, was I could start with a clean sheet,' says Stuart Hepburn. 'I wrote lines for him I love. When he comes in, he says to Fraser, "I've got nothing against shirt-lifters, but I hate sloppy dressers." That summed him up. He was kind of politically correct but politically incorrect. A modern Jim Taggart.

'In my mind, when Burke had got the job, he'd had a look at their files and he'd seen Fraser was gay and from the beginning he wanted to make it clear he had nothing against "poofs", but that he needed people to do the job. He wasn't going to be a caveman, but he wasn't going to be a softy, either.'

'I think it is a good story for all of us because we all got a chance to show our feelings,' comments Blythe. 'And because it was Burke's first one, we saw how the dynamic of that was going to work and it moved things on.'

'I'd watched Alex from *Gregory's Girl* onwards, but I'd never worked with him,' says Colin McCredie. 'I felt that someone of Alex's stature coming on to *Taggart* was a massive vote in confidence for the rest of us. We make *Taggart* up in Scotland and we sometimes forget what the real world thinks of it. Alex had worked for thirty years doing different jobs, but he was coming here saying, "Oh, this is brilliant."'

As the new boy on the block, and with much riding on how the audience would accept him in the role, Alex might have been feeling the pressure. However, the actor seemed to take it in his stride, immediately fitting into the show's established way of doing things, including sharing the Winnebago with the other principal actors.

'There was some trepidation on my part about how I would be accepted in this company, but they couldn't be more welcoming,' he says. 'I was just so used to finishing a job and then you were gone. There were very few things I'd done that were series, and the last one I'd done was a thing called *Back Up* and after it I'd thought, "I never want to do a series again." But on *Taggart* they couldn't have been more pleasant and that just eased the transition. I really enjoyed working with them.'

Of 'Death Trap' he says, proudly, 'It was wonderful, wasn't it? And it looked like a movie. I was knocked out by just how amazing it looked. They gave us a DVD and I went round to John Michie's and we sat down in trepidation and put it on. Within ten minutes I forgot I was nervous, I was completely captivated by it – we both were. And at the end we both looked at each other and said, "That's fantastic."'

'I wrote lines for him I love. When he comes in, he says to Fraser, "I've got nothing against shirt-lifters, but I hate sloppy dressers."'

Chapter 10

Behind the Scenes

A small army of dedicated, hard-working professionals systematically murder dozens of people in Glasgow each year. But they aren't bloodthirsty villains who will stop at nothing to get what they want; they are success-hungry television production professionals who will stop at nothing to achieve their goal ... which is to make some of the best and most gruesome whodunits on the box.

Opposite: Behind the scenes in 'The Ties That Bind', 2005.

Taggart later from Sc 113
Jardine and Reid later from Sc 112

188

SCENE 1...

INT. F

DAY 10

TAGGART
JOAN MA
ALBUMS.
JARDINE

TAGGART
So. Y

JARDINE
We did ...
knew Agi
Both had
Both los

Sc 116   Day ⓪

TAGGART

Sc 116   Day ⑩

Sc 116   DAY ⑩

A family murder.

direct cont into Sc 125

Taggart, Jardine and Reid.

CONTD.

To ensure scenes slip seamlessly into one another, Jardine, Reid and Taggart are photographed for continuity.

Getting the script right
Script editors: Mike Ellen and Denise Paul

Mike and Denise are the link between the scriptwriters and the producers. They help the writers develop their script, making sure it makes sense as well as taking care of more practical considerations, like checking it is long enough.

Mike: 'In *Taggart* we always start with the "world". The characters haven't got much life out of their work – they are good cops, but they aren't incredibly brainy. The point is, they are universal characters who then go into a "world" where some horrible murderer lurks. We show off that world, give an insight into it, while depicting it as being as horrible and suspicious as possible. There is something voyeuristic about it, in a way. You are seeing the way other people live.

'I suspect when the show first started, there was much less of a collaborative process, and writers like Glenn Chandler would have worked to their own method.

'I think Glenn was doing strong plotting, but he would only have been working with the producer Robert Love. Our process involves more people – the writer, script editors, producer and executive producer – but it is similar in that we start with a paragraph, then a couple of pages, before committing to that "world" and the general idea.

'*Taggart* isn't realistic, but we usually have murderers who have real motivation, rather than just pulled like rabbits out of hats. It makes the story seem more real if the writer makes the effort to clarify everyone's actions.'

Denise: 'Sometimes a writer will come to us with an idea, sometimes it is an idea for a "world" which we like, and then we say which of our characters we'd like to have the biggest drive in that story.

'Sometimes, though, the "world" comes from us; we'll suggest something to a writer based on a news story, something we think is exciting, and they will go off and develop it.

'When Graeme Gordon and Eric Coulter inherited the show in 2001, their idea was to give it more of a grounding in reality. It had begun to look like Anytown – the whodunits were all set in big houses and on the outskirts. But people want to watch *Taggart* and say, "That's Glasgow."

'The *Taggart* cops are cops who go on their instincts. People see themselves in our cops. Jackie is the kind of person they could have a blether with.

'What we like today is to have all the characters who are suspects up and running in part one. That is so somebody in the audience can start to figure out who might be the murderer along with the detectives.

'Beyond that, I want characters I can invest in and a good story that surrounds them.'

Ian Madden directs John Michie and Colin McCredie.

The right direction
Director: Ian Madden

'It's not generally different from what you do on any film; it's just a bit tighter. We have less time. It's five weeks' prep; it used to be more. Everything used to be more: the budget used to be bigger – it has got tighter over the years.

'It's an eighteen-day shoot, three five-day weeks and one three-day week, though you sometimes have to shoot those last two days, too. It depends how complicated the script is.

'The plot is the most difficult thing: a whodunit is just very difficult. It's a puzzle, and when you start unpicking it, you are destroying other stuff. It's

In the director's chair. 'Users and Losers', 2007.

The 'Users and Losers' crew earning their keep.

a lot harder than people think it is, especially when you are setting up three or four different suspects and red herrings. It's easy for a writer to tie himself in knots a bit, so you have to unpick it and work out what does work. Is it a viable red herring? If not, can you work on it and get it better?

'You have to shoot four minutes a day on *Taggart*, which is actually fairly generous on television terms now for an episodic drama. But *Taggart* is a bit more ambitious than a lot of episodic dramas. We are trying to shoot it like a film, with the camera on a dolly a lot, even if there is a lot of hand-held. In *The Bill*, for instance, there are a lot of scenes in the canteen with people talking their faces off in between the exciting bits. *Taggart* isn't like that. It's much more of a story, a mystery thriller.'

Morbid but fun
Hair and make-up designer: Karen Campbell

'As a make-up artist, it is the murders that keep *Taggart* fresh for you. It sounds a bit morbid, but we see them as a challenge.

'A while ago we had a serial killer who slashed pentagrams on to the backs of his victims' bodies ["Cause to Kill", 2005]. We had to get the

'It is the murders that keep *Taggart* fresh for you.'

girl and put a coating on her back, then we had to put the blood inside it. It was quite involved, but actually very enjoyable.

'Burns are interesting. We had one killer who was electrocuting people and we had to work out how their feet and hands would be burned and blistered ["Fearful Lightning", 1999].

'Another killer used an acetylene torch ["Dead Man Walking", 2005] to effectively burn his victim's face off. We used gelatine to get that burned-skin effect and you can put the blood underneath it – the skin ends up looking crisp.

'You have to melt the gelatine in a baby's bottle-warmer, then you spread it on to the skin and you can then start putting hair or whatever on to it to make it look as if the skin has been melted off. It is quite safe – just washes off afterwards.

'We've got one episode coming up which is a suffocated victim. But they are talking about doing an extreme close-up so I'm already thinking, "Where can I get contact lenses to give them really dilated pupils?" Because they would give the shot that extra eeriness.

And … action! Blythe Duff takes direction.

Above: The make-up team. It's not as glamorous a job as it sounds.
Below: Another gruesome murder is all in a day's work.

'Strangulations involve more effects there than with a suffocation. You have to do your research so we have forensics books we refer to. They are not that easy to get – they have to be careful who they sell them to because you do get some strange people who would buy this stuff in Waterstone's.

'This book here has some Post-it Notes on the pages – that is to blank out pages we don't like the look of, just in case we flick through and see something horrible by mistake. You want to be prepared to look at some of this stuff.

'But I've also got a contact in Glasgow's Scene of Crime Office – SOCO – who helps us out with queries. I think he wants to be a crime writer himself.

'Occasionally we do pop down and have a visit to the mortuary to chat with a pathologist. I've been offered the chance to look at dead bodies, and to watch an autopsy, but I've always said no. There are some things I still don't want to know.

'But I have seen a relative of mine – but not a gruesome murder. This sounds a bit sick, but I do remember thinking, "Oh, I've been getting it right all these years after all."'

Suits you, sir!
Costume designer: Lesley Abernethy

'The danger is that they are four characters all wearing suits and that therefore they would look the same. But each character is quite different, so we approach what they are wearing differently, too.

'At the start of the year I'll tend to go shopping with each of them. A lot of Colin McCredie's suits come from Next – he has a couple of Paul Smith, but Next seem to hang off him the best. We tend to give him some lighter-coloured shirts – pastels and patterns. He's a bit dandier than Burke or Ross, and he wears ties they would never wear.

'Robbie's suits are often Armani. He's got that rakish personality; he's a bit of a wide boy, and Armani seems to suit his build. It's probably a little bit more expensive than a normal cop would wear, but we're taking a bit of poetic licence there.

'Matt Burke is obviously different again. When I go shopping with him, we go to somewhere like Slater's, the men's outfitters in Glasgow. They tend to sell suits for businessmen: good solid suits. Alex wears a lot of dark colours, too – he's the boss, it looks serious, and it suits him.

'As for Blythe, she's got a mixture of separates and suits. We keep her in trousers – unless the story dictates. We did one where there was some romance going on ["Law", 2006] and we dressed her differently there, a bit softer. But day to day she'll wear trousers and again a lot of black, but also some dark browns, some navy blues and some pinks.

'The problem is, if you buy them all black suits, they'll all appear on set in black, and that doesn't look right. We keep a careful record of who is wearing

what each day, just to make sure there are no obvious clashes. And of course they have to wear the same clothes in scenes that follow on from each other, even though we might film them a week apart.

'We also have to organise costumes for other cast members, too, if necessary. In "Users and Losers" [2007], for instance, I had to find out about what jockeys wear for horse racing. In those situations we just go to a stables and say, "Educate us." It's something we're used to on *Taggart*, as we are often visiting a different "world".'

Wardrobe supervisor: Angela Robertson

'Strathclyde Police keep changing their uniform so we try to keep up as much as we can. They've recently started using a short baton, and we're waiting to get those. We buy the clothes from them. The thing to notice is that they are all the one number: Y147. We're not allowed anything else, otherwise we could get accused of impersonating a police officer.

'The basic uniform is a woolly jumper, shirt and tie in the police station.

Outside, we add a nylon cycle top and/or a waterproof jacket. We also have the Kevlar vests – the bulletproof vests – only ours don't have the Kevlar plates in them, so they wouldn't stop any bullets.

'We've got enough here in stock to dress maybe fifteen or sixteen police at any one time, and there are more in storage to give us different sizes. Plus we have all the equipment belts and the helmets: the helmets are the only difference between the WPC and the PC uniforms.'

Prop picker
Production buyer: Mike Ireland

'I am responsible for buying in props for the production. For this episode, for instance ["Users and Losers", 2007], I got the horses. I had to make sure they were the right size and would look OK together and that our actor could ride one of them.

'A very unusual request was a hat and coat-stand with antler horns so that Fish, who was playing a character for us ["Skin Deep", 2000], could get impaled on it. For something like that, you either have to find it or, at the last resort, make it. I think we found those antlers and then we adapted them.

'Another one was a big statue of the scales of justice – we got one of those at a jumble sale.

'We often go on eBay to get things. We needed a pair of Sap gloves ["A Taste of Money", 2005]; they're leather gloves with bits of lead shot on the knuckles, and I got them over the Internet. I'm not a hundred per cent sure how legal they are, but they were just used as props!'

Prop pickers get all sorts of unusual requests.

It's a dog's life
Animal handler: David Stewart

'There's often a gulf between the artistic side and the animal side and I try to bridge that gap.

'My first *Taggart* was a long time ago: "Gingerbread" [1993]. There was a character in that who was an old woman in a cottage – she was meant to be like a witch – and she had a cat. I was looking after a dog that was visiting the cottage garden and finding things – a human hand. We needed a black cat, but my cat had white paws, so I remember having to dye its feet. The dye didn't really work out, but nobody complained the cat had lilac paws.'

Lewis Foster: a *Taggart* camera operator for twenty years – and loving every minute of it.

Life through a lens
Camera operator: Lewis Foster

'I worked on the first *Taggart*, *Killer* [1983]. Back then we used to film outside on film, but inside the studio we used video cameras. That is why the interior and exterior shots look very different.

'The first one we did all on film was "The Killing Philosophy" [1987]. The cop shop in those days was a former engineering company on South Street [on the Clydeside], but I think it has been demolished now. The last one I did of the old ones was "Gingerbread" [1993], and my little girl, Heather Foster, played one of the children.

'I was a camera assistant at first. In those days we didn't have as many bodies: the camera assistant did the focus and loaded the magazines. Now we've got a focus puller and a loader and usually a trainee – and the grip as well, so it is usually a big department, about six of us. Whereas before it was two plus the grip.

'In those days it still seemed a novelty to have a film crew out in the city. We used to get big crowds gathering round us, and often almost get over run because we'd not have the security guys we have now. I remember on one of the schemes during the summer, we were fine in the morning, but by the afternoon word had got round and we had a sea of kids all round the encampment. They had to drive Mark off with kids hanging off the back of his car. It was like he was a pop star. He was that popular.

'We'd also just go and film where we wanted, without really preparing the way we do now or asking permission. I remember filming in the middle of the Kingston Bridge once – you wouldn't do that now.

'We've done some gory, horrible murders. I remember in "The Killing Philosophy" [1987], a man is killed by "the Bowman" and it was scripted that he was shot with an arrow through the neck, and the killer is watching him die and enjoying this happen. We filmed it and it was really very graphic…but they had to cut a few frames out of it because it was too much for the network. We were always trying to keep things contemporary and to do as much as possible.'

'We've done some gory, horrible murders.'

Keeping It Real
Production designer: Marius van der Werff

Marius worked on *Killer* (1983) and the original series of *Taggart*, before going on to work on other STV productions. He rejoined the show on a regular basis in 2000.

'My department supply the backdrop for the scenes. We research the areas we will be using; we take pictures of real offices, build up a picture of what these offices look like and then create a set which reflects that, but which also looks interesting, giving just enough information on screen to suggest to people what the set is about. We are in the process at the moment of designing the new police set, because we are moving halfway through this year's filming.

'It gives us an opportunity to upgrade the set, to create more physical space, but it will be essentially the same thing.

'When I worked on the first episodes of *Taggart*, the whole look of the place was different. The offices are now technology-based – everyone has a computer, the lighting has changed. It is user-friendly and open. In the early

The *Taggart* team get to grips with their paperwork.

1980s it seemed much more secretive, lots of small offices. We now film all of *Taggart* – as opposed to taping the interiors and using film inserts – and it looks more real. That is why we use real locations as much as possible. They are far more convincing than anything we can create in the studio.

'One of the silliest moments I remember was a Mark McManus episode, "Fatal Inheritance" [1993], when Mark had to sit in a mud bath. Unfortunately, we couldn't get him to sink – it was too liquid – so his tummy kept rising up to the surface. We kept adding muck, hoping his body would sink eventually. It didn't work, so we had to weigh him down using swimmer's weights. Mark was extremely patient throughout – he knew the score and was well liked by the crew.'

The Extra's Diary

'I want to be murdered.'

Well, let's face it, if you're going to be a *Taggart* extra for a day, you *want* to be killed. Preferably in a brutal, sadistic way that involves a lot of blood.

'That might be tricky,' producer Graeme Gordon said with a frown. 'Corpses are very popular. Actually, I'd love to cast famous British celebrities as our victims one day – I think people would love to see Terry Wogan murdered in *Taggart*.'

I take his point, but get him to promise he'll at least try to kill me off. And in my head I begin to imagine life after the episode goes out: being murdered on *Taggart* might lead to other shows, perhaps film work. I make gagging noises and pull faces in front of the mirror as practice. Am I blue enough?

But then, remarkably quickly, the phone rings and Linda in the production office offers me my big break. Only it's not quite the news I was after.

'So how am I done in?' I ask. 'Bludgeoned to death with my own shoe? Hung by my tie from the Erskine Bridge? Chopped up and served as antipasti in a dodgy Italian eatery in the Gorbals?'

'No, I'm sorry,' she replies. 'You're not going to be killed. The murders we're doing right now all need you to be able to speak on camera, and as you are not a member of Equity, you can't.'

I groan with disappointment. My life saved by red tape.

'But it's quite a nice role,' she assures me. 'You're going to be the first vet at the racecourse.'

'The first vet?' Well, at least I'm not the last.

> **'I think people would love to see Terry Wogan murdered in *Taggart*.'**

'I want to be murdered.'

21 April, 9.30 a.m.

Although I opted to drive myself the hour or so from Glasgow to Ayr Racecourse, I'd been a bit nervous about finding the location on time. I needn't have worried, however, as there are bright-pink 'unit' signs all over the place. I'd always had the impression these shoots were 'secret' – it would be harder not finding the moon.

I'm about an hour early. Location work on *Taggart* is usually under way by breakfast, but today they have to wait until the racecourse is up and running before they can film. A steward directs me to the production's travelling village – wardrobe van, canteen, Winnebagos, offices – at the far end of the car park.

They'd told me to dress in 'an appropriate manner' and so I'd carefully picked out my outfit the night before after trying loads of different things on. But now I'm feeling a bit of a prat as I've almost certainly overdone it. In place of my usual jeans and T-shirt, I've gone for heavy-duty cords, waxed jacket and wellingtons. Still, the morning is cloudy and there is a definite chill to the air, so I'll probably appreciate the warmth later.

9.45 a.m.

Angela in wardrobe approves of my outfit with a wry smile. *Taggart* is a contemporary show, so there isn't the pomp and ceremony about wardrobe that you have on a period piece. Angela's job is mainly about managing the various police uniforms and making sure the principals' suits fit. What does she think of the wellies?

'Good. Uh huh.' She nods.

Is it just me, or is she laughing?

She takes a Polaroid so there is a record of what I am wearing. I look like a refugee from a young farmers' picnic.

10 a.m.

Neil Murray, the assistant to the location manager, calls for the extras to gather round for a pep-talk.

D'ye ken?

'We always want to come and do what we want to do – the racecourse in "Users and Losers" [2007] was mainly out of our control and that is something we are not used to. It was also the most expensive venue I've ever had to pay for,' says locations manager Beverley Syme.

'We probably had sixty crew in total at Ayr; it would be less if we were filming in a house in the West End. Here we have more extras and a second camera crew, because we are filming while the event is carrying on.

'The weather can be a pain, but we don't really have the time to worry about it. We're used to rain on *Taggart*.'

This is an unusual day: *Taggart* seldom has more than a handful of extras while filming, but today there are over thirty. Many have dressed for a day at the races – big hats, high-heeled shoes. Nobody else is wearing wellies, though.

The rules are simple: listen for instructions, be patient, be very patient.

I glance at the call sheet and feel a weird sense of pride that I'm listed as 'extra no. 1'.

10.15 a.m.

I corner Karen in the make-up wagon and ask when she needs me. Incredibly, I don't need any make-up at all! I can only assume this is down to my perfect complexion.

10.30 a.m.

Ayr Racecourse is small, but this is its big weekend: the Scottish Grand National takes place the next day. Everything is freshly painted and gleaming. Apart from us, there are quite a few punters already knocking about, but the real business of the races won't get under way for a while yet. In the meantime, *Taggart* director Ian Madden plans to shoot a scene in which the show's 'character horse' and jockey walk round the paddock with other horses. The extras are to perform

'The horse is getting more screen time than me.'

Passing the time of day with producer Graeme Gordon.

as a crowd – only I've not to be included as they plan to use me for a later scene.

It occurs to me that the horse is getting more screen time than me. But it's stupid to be jealous at this stage in my career.

11.30 a.m.

I'm impressed by the good spirits the crew are in – everyone seems happy, relaxed but efficiently busy. They are working in what is essentially a public space, but no one is fazed by comments from passers-by.

'Whit you doin'?'
'Filming *Taggart*.'
'Naw!'

Nobody hangs about for long, though, and I can see why: it's not much of a spectacle. I lose count of how many times the horse is led in and walked around as Alex Norton and Blythe Duff, two of the most recognisable faces in Scotland, weave their way through the extras-enhanced crowd almost unnoticed. Still, at least it's sunny, and between takes my fellow extras and I can lie on the grass and eat ice creams.

12 NOON

A photographer from the Daily Record turns up and asks Alex Norton to do a picture alongside the racecourse's bronze statue of Red Rum, whose name is of course 'Murder' written backwards – allowing the journalist to file a story with the line 'There's been a Red Rum.'

Meanwhile, I get chatting to Jerry Hankin, another extra, and discover he is second vet. Going by age, however, Jerry is definitely the senior man at the practice. A retired dry-cleaner, he lives nearby in Ayr. This is his third *Taggart*, as he's already performed the role of 'passer-by' in the city centre and a 'university lecturer', although all he's seen of himself on the television screen has been part of a bag he was carrying.

1 P.M.

Alex Norton and actor Garry Sweeney, who plays ex-druggie Panda Rammage, row on a path near the paddock. He's so natural, Alex. I must remember when it comes to my scene to try and be like that. The people walking past would be entirely forgiven for thinking he was a real policeman having a row with someone.

Mind you, I guess the camera crew standing a few feet away are a bit of a giveaway.

2 P.M.

It's us. The scene is devilishly tricky, a multi-layered, highly choreographed gem that takes place in some trees outside the stables. Jerry and I are in conference with Reid (Duff) while Burke (Norton) confronts a suspect fifteen feet away in the foreground. 'Now, remember,' Jerry tells me, 'don't look at the camera.'

But first a rehearsal: we vets act our socks off, improvising vet-like lines like we were the stars of a Mike Leigh version of All Creatures Great and Small. 'The hoof was bruised,' we prattle, and 'His fetlock was broken in three places.' Fortunately, no microphone picked any of this up, otherwise we'd probably be sacked. Then Reid says, 'Thank you, gentlemen,' and turns to join her boss, who is shouting blue murder at Panda. At which point I feel myself looking directly at the camera. Doh!

2.10 P.M.

We're ready to go again. Blythe takes up her position once more. There's a wee delay as Alex discusses some point with Ian, the director. I can't follow it, but it's probably about the inner turmoil Burke is sensing right now in the script, his emotional centre. Either that or, like me, he's wondering what happened to lunch.

D'ye ken?

Jim Taggart wouldn't have been impressed. Mike Jardine would probably have sneered. And it is unlikely that Burke, Reid, Ross or Fraser are aware of the fact, otherwise they would have done something about it by now, too. The thing is, there's a wee spy in Glasgow CID, and he keeps sneaking into places he shouldn't be.

Karen Campbell, the hair and make-up designer, explains, 'He's called Dennis K. Roo. It's a little kangaroo.'

A *what*?

'*Taggart* fans can look for him, as he gets on the set quite a lot. The costume girls made him a tiny SOCO suit – the overalls the police wear in a scene of crime. And for one show ["The Ties That Bind", 2005], which was about S&M, they made him a gimp outfit.'

I find it hard to believe that Scotland's four most eminent detectives would fail to notice a kangaroo dressed in black leather and chains.

'He's only a few inches high,' laughs Karen. 'He is sometimes in the lab, or someone's desk. I'm not sure how aware of them they are high up. But he's started travelling as well. We would send him on different jobs. He went up to *Monarch of the Glen* wearing a tam-o'-shanter. And he met Scarlett Johansson in London for *Match Point,* but he declined to meet Woody Allen. And then he was in the Tour de France wearing a yellow jersey and cycling goggles. He's even met Lorraine Kelly.'

Costume designer Lesley Abernethy takes up the story: 'Dennis is always hanging around with famous people. He's met John Sessions, Burt Kwouk, from the *Pink Panther* movies, and Brian Capron. His favourite outfit is probably the kilt we had made for him. He's very patriotic about Scotland – for a kangaroo.'

Lights. Camera. Action. We're finally ready to go.

We've been told that rather than breaking for a trip to the canteen, we're to grab something as we go along. But I'm starving.

We chat to Blythe to take our mind away from our rumbling stomachs. 'We're Tom and Jerry,' laughs second vet, before going on to talk about his dry-cleaning business. Blythe actually remembers his old shop and laments how hard it is to find a decent dry-cleaner in Glasgow.

2.15 P.M.

Suddenly we're off; this time it's a real take. James Macpherson told me a story once about doing a scene in a hospital where the extra lying on a bed was attached to a heart monitor. As soon as the director said, 'Action,' his heart rate went sky high, setting off an alarm. Mark McManus had apparently said to him, 'We have to do that fifty times a day.'

Well, right now I know exactly what that story is all about. My heart is pounding as my image is consigned to digital video: me, in conversation with Jackie Reid.

I'm proud of myself because this time I don't look at the camera. 'His hoof was very red, as if he'd stood on a pea,' I find myself saying. Where does this stuff come from? No wonder telly writers are well paid. Someone says cut, but then – we have to go again as Alex Norton has stumbled over a word from the actual script. 'Remembering your lines is easy,' Blythe says. 'It's saying them in the right order that's often difficult.'

Cheers! Colin and John enjoy a pint.

2.30 P.M.

We shoot again. Each time we've done this scene, for real and in the rehearsals, Blythe seems to move away from us quicker. Maybe I'm being paranoid, or maybe she can't take any more of our fetlock banter. But then, as Jerry points out, we are about as important to the plot as the tree we are standing under.

2.35 P.M.

Job done, we relocate to the winner's enclosure for the next scenes. It takes a short time for Madden to set up his crews. He's using two cameras, and shooting in the midst of the crowd. The finished product should look extremely realistic – because everything around us is real. It's a really glam crowd – lots of women in heels, men in suits. And in the VIP area every table seems to have a bottle of champagne. Extras are placed here and there about to fill in some gaps, but as the race meeting is now well under way, it hardly seems necessary. It's incredible how relaxed people are around the cameras. Even when John Michie and Colin McCredie appear to quiz a jockey, all you get are a few curious glances.

> **D'ye ken?**
>
> On set when lunch is called, the principal actors are served first – or food is collected for them by assistant directors. Then the crew get their meals, followed by the extras.

3 P.M.

I've been told I can't leave until the director signs off my scene, which makes me feel terribly important.

'The director has to sign me off!'

Actually, the director barely knows I'm alive, but there is an outside chance they'll decide to reshoot

OK, I'm bored now.

the sequence so I have to stay put. In fact, all the extras have to stay in the vicinity, but it is clear they won't get much to do for a while. As one tells me, 'Sometimes they only use you for a few hours; other times, like now, it is the whole day, but the fee is the same.' Few grumble, however, as the weather is now glorious, and with the racing in full swing, there's plenty to bet on. John Michie causes a stir among the crew by backing a series of winners.

3.30 P.M.

OK, now we are getting a bit bored. It's too hot, my ice cream melted, and the stewards won't let me into the VIP area. I slink off and buy a burger.

4 P.M.

A group of extras are rounded up by one of the assistant directors, who explains they want to do some second-unit filming in the grandstand. Once there, I'm advised to stay out of shot – again – because it would look odd for my 'character' to crop up in a different context, though secretly I wonder to myself if the director has taken a dislike to my wellingtons. I stand and watch the others cheer and clap on order, to the amusement of the real-life punters standing around them. 'Don't film me,' shouts one guy from behind his pint glass. 'I called into work sick this morning!'

5.30 P.M.

I'm finally told I can go home. I trudge back to the car, where the first thing I do is change my shoes.

3 January 2007, 9 P.M.

This is it. The first new *Taggart* of the year, and it's 'Users and Losers', Episode 81, starring Blythe Duff, Alex Norton, John Michie, Colin McCredie – and me.

I text everyone I know: 'I'm in tonight's *Taggart*.'
Everyone I know texts me back: 'Are you murdered?'
I text everyone I know: 'No. I'm a– Never mind. Just watch it.'

The show goes on at the racecourse – but without me.

It's a cracking episode. Ian Madden kicks things off with a brutal attack in a city-centre back lane: a man is literally booted to death. These scenes are intercut with shots of Ayr Racecourse from the day I was there... but, no, you can't see me.

The plot weaves its way along: Burke is playing the good Samaritan at a drugs rehab centre, people are bumped off, a jockey is having it away with the wife of his boss, next thing is she's killed, and there's that bloke Panda looking as dodgy as undercooked sliced sausage.

Omigod, they're at the racecourse. There's a horse being looked at by the vets. This is it. Deep breath.

And... that was it. It's gone. I wasn't there. They never used me.

Instead of Blythe Duff speaking to Jerry and me, all we got was a jump shot between a close-up of Burke and a close-up of her. No question it works nicely as a scene: it's tight, to the point and dramatic...

But it doesn't include me!

Deflated, I sink into the sofa. Fame will have to wait.

Perhaps next time they'll let me be the gloved hand.

Chapter 11

A Brave New *Taggart*

After the success of 'Death Trap' (2002) there was no resting on laurels for the *Taggart* team. Since the broadcast of the first Matt Burke episode, there have been thirty-five new whodunits, with four more in production for 2008. Even with DCI Matt Burke in charge, Glasgow has never been more dangerous.

Opposite: DCI Burke alone with just a Glasgow backdrop and his thoughts in 'The Ties That Bind'.

'Is this the smell of napalm in the morning, or a waste of my valuable time?'

When Burke arrives at the scene of a suspicious fire at the beginning of 'Fire, Burn' (2002), he quickly sets his priorities. 'Is this the smell of napalm in the morning, or a waste of my valuable time?' he barks, before immediately ordering Fraser to go and get him a black coffee and bacon roll from a nearby caff. 'Make sure the bacon is like this place,' he adds. 'Done to a crisp.'

But while his stomach might be grumbling, the new DCI remains utterly focused. Indeed, it is Jackie Reid's attitude he doesn't like.

Although never a soap, *Taggart* always recognises the developments and experiences of its main characters. 'Fire, Burn' was broadcast just a month after Jardine's death, and the loss is still strongly felt. For Reid, he was more than just a colleague: she is mourning a friend and beginning to question whether the job that killed him is something she wants to carry on doing. She is also at odds with her husband, DCI Brian Holmes, who wants her to quit Glasgow for a desk job in London, or perhaps a more domesticated arrangement. As a result, sparks fly in confrontations with her new boss. 'The king is dead, long live the king,' Burke tells her during one row. 'Life goes on and so does crime. I can't afford to be with people who don't want to be in my team.'

Reid's self-doubt is set against a highly dangerous investigation. A rogue bomber, calling himself 'the Taxman' is terrorising businesses and demanding huge pay-offs in protection money. To succeed in catching their killer, Reid and Burke have to settle their differences and come to terms with one another. In truth, Burke is far from impressed by the long-serving DS, who DI Robbie Ross has assured him is an excellent detective. However, when the two of them must defuse a bomb together – and come within a wire of blowing themselves up – respect is won. There's a telling moment when Reid puts the screws on one suspect, getting out more information than Burke expected. He begins to see her in a new light. Not that the ghost of Jardine or the issues surrounding the new boss are immediately resolved.

'Fire, Burn', written by John Brown, also introduces Sheila Crombie, played by Scots actress Tamara Kennedy. The simmering flirtation between the forensic specialist and the DCI is there for all to see, and it takes a while for Reid to become accustomed to it. Not that there's much chance of the relationship turning *Taggart* into a workplace romance – as Burke tells Ross in the pub, 'I used to be married, I used to have a family, that's all you need to know.' Even so, the close bond between Burke and the scientist grates with Reid, who isn't used to playing second fiddle to anyone in an investigation. The tension resurfaces during later shows.

What a way to go

In 'Watertight' (2002), launderette manager Sadie McPhail (Rae Hendrie) is murdered and her body hidden in a tumble-drier. When the team arrive at the scene, they hear her rolling around in the drum. It is the only time in *Taggart* that someone has been murdered by a tumble-drier.

The same year saw two further two-hour episodes: 'Watertight' and 'The Friday Event'.

In the first of these, it is Robbie's turn to test the patience of his boss. A prostitute is found murdered in Kelvingrove Park, in the city's West End. When CCTV footage identifies a likely suspect, Robbie behaves as if he has something to hide. Working with his own informant, he brings the murder inquiry under threat. This is classic Ross – well intentioned but maverick. Fortunately, he makes amends, eventually figuring out the identity of the real killer.

Burke and Reid feel the tension in 'Death Trap', 2002.

Hidden depths

Burke exhibits knowledge and charm hitherto unknown in the third *Taggart* of 2002. 'The Friday Event' is a gothic masterpiece that harks back to the show's vintage period in the 1980s. Investigating the murder of a teenage boy at a top Glasgow school, suspicion first falls on a drug dealer before two other extraordinary murders take place that are rooted in the art world.

Burke is clearly a no-nonsense, meat-and-potatoes man, but when the inquiry calls for him to get on the good side of a famous Glasgow painter, Eddie Drummond (John Kay Steel), he reveals a knowledge of art that is surprising, and a degree of charm that would rival Robbie Ross on a date with a dream blonde.

The murders themselves are careful recreations of scenes from paintings by the French painter Jacques-Louis David: 'Death of Marat' and 'Andromache Mourning Hector'. When he realises this, the DCI is able to mutter the immortal line 'They're both neoclassical: it's the art teacher!'

For the next series, however, ITV was to ask SMG to change the *Taggart* format and commissioned six episodes to run over sixty minutes, plus one of 120 minutes. For *Taggart* this was new territory, but Eric Coulter and Graeme Gordon didn't balk at the task. Because of adverts, the new format meant about forty-six minutes of actual screen time – and a change of pace.

In a sense, this new format reflected a wider move in television towards shorter American-style episodes. It called for efficient yet well crafted stories, which the *Taggart* team set about delivering.

The shows that ran in December 2002 and January 2003 showed that SMG were highly capable of turning out high-quality episodes of *Taggart* whatever the restrictions. 'Hard Man' (2002) is set in a beleaguered shipyard on the Clyde and captures a sense of the passion and high stakes working on the river can still generate in Glasgow. 'Fade to Black' (2002) is a creepy tale about a nurse apparently murdered by a stalker who has been photographing her obsessively – only for Burke to realise, after some diligent work by Sheila Crombie, that the death is linked to a series of drug overdoses.

In 'Blood Money' (2002), the simmering tensions between Reid and Burke come to the fore again when she is excluded from a boys' night at the boxing. But when the fight promoter is found killed the next morning, a bundle of cash stuffed in his mouth, she pulls more than her fair share of the weight in the investigation.

'New Life' (2003) features a spectacular car bombing that kills a leading genetic scientist, while 'Bad Blood' (2003) is about gangland rivalries and internal treachery. In 'Halfway House' (2003), while the team investigate a series of killings relating to a hostel, Reid reveals she has split from her husband and is no longer wearing his ring.

The run reached its climax with the two-hour feature length 'An Eye for an Eye' (2003). With twice as much time to develop a storyline and characters, this plot about the murders of two doctors from a high-profile women's health clinic is a definite high point. Lesley Harcourt, who goes on to play forensics

> **Classic Fraser:**
> 'That's a poinsettia; I bought my auntie one for Christmas.'
> 'Atonement' (2003)

specialist Gemma Kerr, appears for the first time as Dr Roberta Paton, and almost gets her head blown off in the first minute by a shotgun as she enters a booby-trapped office.

The more involved story sees Fraser sorely tested. While on duty to protect one of the doctors, he falls asleep and wakes to find she has been murdered – brutally strung up in a tree in her garden. Burke is furious and puts him on suspension. His career is very much on the line. Only towards the end of the adventure does Reid prove her colleague had been drugged and that the real killer was far closer to home than anyone had by that time expected.

Sex and death

Taggart would return twice more in 2003, but this time ITV requested another change to the running time. The series would now be filmed for a ninety-minute slot – which allowed for some more elaborate plotting, without any loss of pace – a format that would persist until 2008.

'Penthouse and Pavement' (2003) is a deliciously devised yarn, which starts with the murder of a well-known horror writer, Jason Randell (Steve Hamilton) – strangled while having sex with a prostitute in a back alley behind his hotel. The prostitute survives, only to be murdered later after providing some tantalisingly cryptic clues as to the identity of the killer.

The story captures the high-to-low society spectrum *Taggart* has long excelled at: Randell's wife sips tea in the conservatory, while the prostitutes her husband frequented barter for a living on the 'drag'. And it introduces Gemma Kerr, the new youthful forensics expert, who is quick to figure out the way Randell met his death. While she sends Robbie Ross's head spinning during a re-enactment, Reid has to overcome some vehement anti-police prejudices if she is to help protect Glasgow's sex workers, who appear to be the target of a serial killer.

In the next episode, 'Atonement' (2003), the focus shifts back on to Burke when an old case comes back to haunt him. The show marked *Taggart's* twentieth anniversary, and fittingly the crime at the centre of the intrigue is the same vintage. When Billy McCree is found dead in his workshop – his hand sawn off and a red rose left by his body – suspicion naturally falls on the man he helped put away, bank robber Jim Naysmith. However, although recently released from prison and working in a local florist's, Naysmith has a cast-iron alibi for the crime, leading the team to pursue other possible motives. The climax of the mystery comes with a memorable stand-off between the killer and Burke, who looks set to be executed until Ross, Reid and Fraser arrive with armed support.

'Emotionally, it was a lovely episode. You saw the actors come through and make a really good job there.'

Fans would only get two new *Taggart* episodes during 2004, but 'Compensation' and 'Saints and Sinners' would keep interest keen while ITV opted to repeat older shows.

Burke reveals more about his past in the first of these, a story about the grim realities of farming in the aftermath of the foot and mouth crisis. 'He befriends this old farmer,' Alex Norton explains. 'That was the first glimpse of Burke's background and that his relationship with his father was difficult. His father wanted him to do one thing, and Burke wanted to do something else. That chimed with me because that was very much my own situation with my dad.'

'Saints and Sinners', broadcast in December 2004, in which a top lawyer is found murdered, kicked off a series of six new episodes running into February 2005, and were followed by a further seven to be shown later the same year. *Taggart's* ability to pull in a solid audience had never been in more demand.

It's an extremely creative period for the team, and one that sees various developments for each of the characters. Notably, Reid steps out from the shadows of her past and reasserts herself as a leading player in the team. In 'Puppet on a String' (2005), she goes undercover to expose a hit man – a scenario that includes the hilarious tease that she is

Reid goes undercover to prove her worth to Burke in 'Puppet on a String', 2005.

actually on a romantic night out with Burke. However, their dinner date, complete with a chilled bottle of New World chardonnay and the rare sight of the detective wearing a skirt, is only for the benefit of a camera. 'A kiss would help,' suggests a WPC. 'Aye, now you're pushing it,' sniffs Reid in response.

But Reid is feeling more secure about herself. 'She is in a better place now to deal with Burke – there's no big deal, he's just the boss,' comments Blythe. 'Of all the characters, she's the one who can stand up to him. I think she's got a soft spot for him, too. And because she's comfortable in her own skin, she doesn't hold back. It's hard to know whether I've injected that in her because I'm like that or whether it's in there from the writer.'

However, Reid still had issues to deal with from her past: the loss of Jardine as a friend, the marriage she perhaps rushed into. In 'Mind Over Matter' (2005), it emerges that she has attended counselling, and agrees to do so again in order to gather information about a murder. However, she reaches some closure as the team attempt to track down an apparently random serial killer in 'A Death Foretold' (2005). It opens with Gemma Kerr wondering if Jackie has a new man in her life. 'Doubt it,' says Robbie. 'There hasn't been a smile on her face for ages.'

The reason for this is kept hidden until well into the story. Reid is preoccupied because her ex-husband, DCI Brian Holmes, is in a hospice dying of cancer and has asked her to keep his plight private from those who know him in the force. Unquestionably, it is one of Blythe's strongest episodes: a cracking whodunit infused with a memorable personal story she handles extremely well. But it also gives the character a fresh start. No longer would her marriage – and by implication, the memory of Mike Jardine – weigh on her.

'I get a lot of compliments for that one,' producer Graeme Gordon says of 'A Death Foretold'. 'Emotionally, it was a lovely episode. You saw the actors come through and make a really good job there.'

Ross lives to fight another day in 'Do or Die', 2005.

Don't worry, darlin', I'll take care of it

Ross is seldom far from the centre of controversy. At the end of 'Atonement' (2003) he puts his boss's life at risk in a face-off with the killer. In 'Compensation' (2004), he spends more time trying to bed the locals than figuring out who the guilty parties are. And in 'The Wages of Sin' (2005), his attempt at going undercover with an organised crime gang ends with his being stripped naked and locked in a pen with the livestock at a turkey farm. Well, he always was one for the birds.

Ross meets his biggest challenge, however, in 'In Camera' (2005), an episode that has proved to be a big favourite of the fans and has been repeated on ITV. It begins with an extremely unusual situation for *Taggart*: a cop we know – Robbie – out on a date with the beautiful Eve Hamilton (Jenny Ryan). They are all over each other, in love. They arrive at a house in the country to stay the night, only there's a dead body in the living room and the first thing they do is make a run for it. After this, he goes out of his way to cover their tracks, fiddles with evidence and even helps her out in the interrogation room. It's utterly compelling because you wonder, 'What is Robbie trying to hide?' When internal affairs crop up asking about an old case of his, you start to suspect the answer is, quite a lot.

'I thought it was a great way to start a *Taggart* with a murder where a detective inspector finds the dead body with his girlfriend and then walks away saying, "Don't worry, I'll sort it out,"' says John Michie. 'You know, sometimes Ross just doesn't get it. With the life experience he's had, you'd think he'd be a bit cleverer, but there's that arrogance to him. He's saying to the girl, "Ah'm a big guy, sweetheart, I'll sort it." But in fact he's being manipulated all the way. I love his old boss in that episode, too. It was nice to go back ten years to when he was a corrupt cop and you saw that's where Robbie got his ways of doing things. But in the end he stands up to his old boss and says, "I'm not like that any more and I'm not going to cover this story up.'"

Ross survives to fight another day, of course, and even joins the army for 'Do or Die', broadcast in December 2005. Obviously, he's only undercover – following a suspicious death in a barracks – but it is a wake-up call for him nevertheless. 'It was fun to film that. Robbie can't keep up with the pace of the other soldiers, so out on a run, he has to hitch a ride back to base,' John recalls. 'In the end, Robbie sticks his neck out; he knows who the killer is but wants to give the guy another chance, because he sees the guy has been manipulated by someone else. That is typical of him: he likes to bend the rules if he sees a reason to do it. But I think it also appealed to a side of him we don't see much of – the fact he is a parent.'

> **Classic Ross:**
>
> 'Kelly, you know I really like you, don't you? But it doesn't mean I won't bring you in for questioning.'
> 'Compensation' (2004)

Ross attempts to take care of things in 'In Camera'.

Fraser's ex-boyfriend provides some rare love interest for the gay detective. 'A Taste of Money', 2005.

Get a life

Ross is, however, very much a lone wolf, as are all the *Taggart* detectives in Glasgow CID. In 'The Caring Game' (2007), family ties impede on his work life, causing him to question his future. But in the end there is no contest: it's career first.

As Blythe says, when it comes to their private lives, 'They are all failures to a degree.' She explains, 'There was a great line in one of the episodes ["Penthouse and Pavement", 2003] that sums us up. Reid says something like, "That's rich coming from three divorcees and a homosexual who never does it."

'It's very true about the police in general. I think if you can keep your family life going and be a detective, then good on you. Most of the time you are not at home, and you don't see your kids growing up. A friend of mine who's got three years to go before he retires from the police force says he's never had a holiday yet without thinking, "Am I going to get on holiday?" And that's in almost twenty years. That's a lot for a partner to put up with.'

Certainly, Fraser's lack of action is noted in 'A Taste of Money' (2005), when an ex-boyfriend is a witness to a particularly grisly murder of a restaurant critic. The attraction is clearly still there between them – although fleeting, it is the young DC's only on-screen

Classic Burke:

'You see yourself as some sort of genius, don't ye? Some kind of criminal mastermind. But the truth is, you're nothing but a low-life murdering scumbag and I'll prove it.'
'Puppet on a String' (2005)

kiss – but it is clearly not a relationship that will be helped by one of them being a cop. In 'Law' (2006), his sense of loneliness is clearly a factor as he takes two young lovers under his wing during an investigation into a murder at a fairground. When he realises he has made an error of judgement, he risks his own life to put it right.

As for Burke, even after more than thirty episodes, he still remains an enigma. In 'Running Out of Time' (2005), he is shot in the neck by a hit man and struggles for his life. It is notable how alone he is in the hospital – no family or partner, just his team from the office hoping that he will pull through. When Ross and Fraser visit his flat, hoping to find a clue as to who the attacker might be, they find an orderly bachelor pad that looks barely slept in.

However, he does open up to a degree in two episodes broadcast in 2007, 'Users and Losers' and 'The Thirteenth Step', when elements about his relationship with his father comes to the fore. In the latter, he finds himself confronted with a retired cop, now a local loan shark, who goads him about his drunken dad.

However, while the *Taggart* detectives often have to confront things about their own past, or their own failings, while chasing a killer, the glimpses we get of their life beyond their jobs is, and will always remain, fleeting.

'I feel too many shows go home with a character, and that doesn't work,' says executive producer Eric Coulter. 'You have to find out about a character in the course of an investigation. So we only drop little bits or pieces – say if we go back to Burke's old neighbourhood, or the investigation involves someone his father knew ["The Thirteenth Step", 2007]. The audience would quite like to know more, but it's a tease: to tell them more would spoil the effect. Once you tell them, it's over.'

'It does what it says on the tin'

In recent years *Taggart* has seen women shoved down stairwells in wheelchairs, body parts sent through the post and a plethora of assassinations by rifle, handgun, knife, electrocution and even crucifixion. Murders have included hard-up housewives, frustrated artists, vengeful bank robbers and devious doctors. Through it all, Burke and the team have bonded, bickered and cut to the chase. The series will continue throughout 2008 – with six more one-hour films ordered by ITV – and beyond. Away from the camera, things have been running smoothly for the show, too.

'They actually get on really well.' Colin and John having a laugh on set.

'The lead actors' Winnebago can be a bit like a student flat,' reflects Eric with a laugh. 'You get tension occasionally – and cheese sandwiches left out to go stale. But actually they get on really well. That's not PR, that's the truth.'

'I like the fact we have some input,' says Blythe. 'That's why I still do the job, otherwise I'd tear my hair out. Plus I get on with the guys. We appreciate each other's talents, know each other and slag each other off – and can actually say if we don't think something works. It's a really good working relationship. It would be silly to say we don't drive each other daft sometimes, but I think that can be healthy.'

'*Taggart* is a really happy ship by and large – people who work here tend to like the show, and though we work hard, we know it's not open-heart surgery,' Eric concurs. 'At the end of the day we do our job the best we can. Sometimes we do have to work a fourteen-hour day. Sometimes it is a lot of hard, dry police dialogue. But when the characters get a personal story they love it because that's when they get a push. All I ask is that people see *Taggart* for what it is: a crime show. Critics sometimes review a meat dish as fish: they'll ask why we have so much plot, and don't dwell on the characters. Well, this is crime; it is about plot. People recognise *Taggart* as well made, well acted and well put together. It does what it says on the tin. It's a whodunit.'

Appendix I
The Episodes

Pilot: *Killer* (6, 13, 20 September 1983)
1.   'Dead Ringer' (2, 9, 16 July 1985)
2.   'Murder in Season' (23, 30 July, 6 Aug 1985)
3.   'Knife Edge' (24 February, 3, 10 March 1986)
4.   'Death Call' (2, 9, 16 September 1986)
5.   'The Killing Philosophy' (15, 22, 29 April 1987)
6.   'Funeral Rites' (9, 16, 23 September 1987)
7.   'Cold Blood' (31 December 1987)
8.   'Dead Giveaway' (7, 14, 21 September 1988)
9.   'Root of Evil' (28 September 1988)
10.   'Double Jeopardy' (30 December 1988)
11.   'Flesh and Blood' (5, 12, 19 September 1989)
12.   'Love Knot' (1 January 1990)
13.   'Hostile Witness' (22 February, 1, 8 March 1990)
14.   'Evil Eye' (4, 11, 18 September 1990)
15.   'Death Comes Softly' (3, 10, 17 December 1990)
16.   'Rogues' Gallery' (31 December 1990)
17.   'Violent Delights' (1 January 1992)
18.   'Nest of Vipers' (9, 16, 23 January 1992)
19.   'Double Exposure' (30 January, 6, 13 February 1992)
20.   'The Hit Man' (17, 24 September, 1 October 1992)
21.   'Ring of Deceit' (8, 15, 22 October 1992)
22.   'Fatal Inheritance' (1 January 1993)
23.   'Death Benefits' (16, 23 February, 2 March 1993)
24.   'Gingerbread' (20, 27 April, 4 May 1993)
25.   'Death Without Dishonour' (11, 18, 25 May 1993)
26.   'Instrument of Justice' (30 September, 7, 14 October 1993)
27.   'Forbidden Fruit' (1 January 1994)
28.   'Secrets' (6, 13, 20 October 1994)
29.   'Hellfire' (27 October 1994)
30.   'Prayer for the Dead' (11, 18, 25 January 1995)
31.   'Black Orchid' (25 February 1995)
32.   'Legends' (26 October, 2, 9 November 1995)
33.   'Devil's Advocate' (4, 11, 18 January 1996)
34.   'Angel Eyes' (21 March 1996)
35.   'Dead Man's Chest' (19 September 1996)
36.   'Apocalypse' (9, 16, 23 January 1997)

49. 'Wavelength' (21 September 2000)
50. 'Football Crazy' (28 September 2000)
51. 'Falling in Love' (1 October 2001)
52. 'Death Trap' (14 January 2002)
53. 'Fire, Burn' (21 January 2002)
54. 'Watertight' (8 July 2002)
55. 'The Friday Event' (15, 16 July 2002)
56. 'Hard Man' (4 December 2002)
57. 'Fade to Black' (11 December 2002)
58. 'Blood Money' (18 December 2002)
59. 'New Life' (4 January 2003)
60. 'Bad Blood' (11 January 2003)
61. 'Halfway House' (18 January 2003)
62. 'An Eye for an Eye' (25 January 2003)
63. 'Penthouse and Pavement' (7 October 2003)
64. 'Atonement' (3 December 2003)
65. 'Compensation' (30 April 2004)
66. 'Saints and Sinners' (30 December 2004)
67. 'Puppet on a String' (6 January 2005)
68. 'The Wages of Sin' (13 January 2005)
69. 'The Ties That Bind' (20 January 2005)
70. 'In Camera' (27 January 2005)
71. 'Mind Over Matter' (3 February 2005)
72. 'Cause and Effect' (16 September 2005)
73. 'A Taste of Money' (23 September 2005)
74. 'A Death Foretold' (30 September 2005)
75. 'Running Out of Time' (4 November 2005)
76. 'Cause to Kill' (11 November 2005)
77. 'Do or Die' (9 December 2005)
78. 'Dead Man Walking' (16 December 2005)
79. 'Law' (22 March 2006)
80. 'The Best and the Brightest' (29 March 2006)
81. 'Users and Losers' (3 January 2007)
82. 'The Thirteenth Step' (17 January 2007)
83. 'Tenement' (1 April 2007)
84. 'Pinnacle' (4 July 2007)
85. 'Genesis' (tbc 2007)
86. 'The Caring Game' (tbc 2007)
87. 'Lifeline' (tbc 2007)

Appendix II
Taggart Around the World

It's a seemingly simple formula that has made *Taggart* Scotland's most successful television export. A total of 141 territories have bought the show historically, with fifty-four currently following the series. In France it is dubbed, in Scandinavia they prefer subtitles, and in Australia they sometimes wish they had them. The formula has even attracted the jealous attention of foreign producers. In Italy there is talk of recreating the series, setting it in Turin or Milan, and translating some of its plots directly into Italian.

There's a whole world out there hungry for a murder or two before bedtime.

'It's the biggest audiovisual export in Scotland. It's comparable to other exports like whisky and shortbread,' says Paul Sheehan, commercial director of SMG Productions.

'We have sales of at least £1.5 million globally this year alone, including a major UK TV deal.

'The other thing is, everyone shares in that money. The writers and actors and people in the production share in it. It is a lot of money that is going back into the Scottish creative community.

'The international market is used to buying series from America where one season lasts twenty-six episodes. One problem British producers often get when it comes to selling shows is foreign buyers say, "We like it, but we need more." Because there are now so many episodes of *Taggart*, broadcasters find it easier to schedule. We're at number eighty-eight now, and many of those are more than one instalment.'

But it isn't just volume that counts. Just as Robert Love in 1983 knew that a detective story would have commercial appeal, so it is that the modern *Taggart* attracts an international audience hungry for a murder or two before bedtime.

'It is a very strong whodunit, a thriller, and that is a strong sell for any channel,' says Sheehan. 'It is the backbone of the schedule in places like Japan. In Denmark they are often more up to date than we are in the UK; they'll show a new *Taggart* as soon as they take delivery of it. By contrast, ITV1 will often have episodes on the shelf for a year or so before screening them.'

John Michie and the *Taggart* crew filming 'A Death Foretold'.

Internationally, *Taggart* is now seen as a competitor with the best of world television: up there with America's multi-million dollar series *CSI* and *NYPD Blue*.

'DVD is one of the things that has worked incredibly well for us,' says Sheehan. 'As well as the UK, it is now available in the Benelux countries, America and Australia. And now there are new media opportunities arriving all the time: video on demand, for instance, is an area we are looking at.'

Taggart isn't just about a murder any more; it's big business. Yet the team are sensitive to the fact that people – especially Scots – sometimes forget just how successful the programme is.

'In the industry in Scotland, people think, "They do *Taggart*, that must be dead easy,"' reflects Eric Coulter, 'because it's not a show that wins awards. But getting a crime plot to work is a lot harder than guessing the murderer while you are watching it.'

'*Taggart* is a real industry employer in this part of the world,' adds Graeme Gordon. 'We've made seven films this past year – that's seven times twenty equals a hundred and forty actors, not including our main four jobs, in one year. Plus a crew of fifty or sixty at any one time. We are the biggest employer in Scotland in terms of crews and actors, I am sure of that.'

'Those seven episodes of *Taggart* have seen us spend about six million in one year,' says Eric. 'If three films had come to Scotland with the same budget, they would have got a lot more coverage than we do. People would be dancing down Sauchiehall Street.'

Where is *Taggart* shown?

Below are the territories that have shown *Taggart*. Those in *italics* screen the programme currently:

1. *Afar (Ethiopia)*
2. Afghanistan
3. African Central Republic
4. Albania
5. *Algeria*
6. *Andorra*
7. Argentina
8. *Australia*
9. Bahrain
10. Bangladesh
11. *Belgium*
12. Belize
13. *Benin*
14. Bhutan
15. Bolivia
16. Bosnia
17. Brazil
18. Brunei
19. Bulgaria
20. *Burkina Faso*
21. Burma
22. Cambodia
23. *Cameroon*
24. Canada
25. Capo d'Istria
26. *Chad*
27. *Channel Islands*
28. Chile
29. China
30. Colombia
31. *Congo Brazzaville*
32. *Corsica*
33. Costa Rica
34. Croatia
35. *Czech Republic*
36. *Denmark*
37. *Djibouti Republic*
38. Ecuador
39. Egypt
40. El Salvador
41. Equatorial Guinea
42. Eritrea
43. *Finland*
44. *France*
45. *French Polynesia*
46. *Futuna Island*
47. *Gabon*
48. *Gambier*
49. Guadeloupe
50. Guatemala
51. Guiana
52. *Guinea*
53. *Herzegovina*
54. Honduras
55. Hong Kong
56. *Hungary*
57. *Iceland*
58. *India*
59. Indonesia
60. Iran
61. Iraq
62. *Ireland*
63. *Isle of Man*
64. *Israel*

65. *Italy*
66. *Ivory Coast*
67. *Japan*
68. Jordan
69. Kuwait
70. Laos
71. Lebanon
72. *Luxembourg*
73. Libya
74. Macau
75. *Madagascar*
76. Malaysia
77. Maldives
78. *Mali*
79. Malta

80. *Marquesas*
81. *Mauritania*
82. *Mauritius*
83. Mexico
84. *Monaco*
85. Mongolia
86. Morocco
87. Nepal
88. *Netherlands*

89. New Caledonia
90. *New Zealand*
91. Nicaragua
92. *Niger*
93. *North America*
94. *Northern Ireland*
95. North Korea
96. North Yemen
97. Norway
98. Pakistan
99. Panama
100. Papua
101. Paraguay
102. Peru
103. Philippines
104. Poland

105. Oman
106. Omar
107. Qatar
108. Republic of South Africa
109. *Reunion Islands*
110. Romania
111. *Russia*
112. San Marino
113. Saudi Arabia
114. *Senegal*
115. Serbia and Montenegro
116. Singapore
117. Slovak Republic
118. Slovenia
119. Somalia
120. South Korea
121. South Yemen
122. Sri Lanka
123. Sudan
124. Sweden
125. *Switzerland*
126. Syria
127. Taiwan
128. Thailand
129. *Togo*
130. *Tunisia*
131. Turkey
132. Turks and Caicos Islands
133. Ukraine
134. United Arab Emirates
135. *United Kingdom*
136. Uruguay
137. Vatican City
138. Venezuela
139. Vietnam
140. *Western Sahara*
141. *Zaire*

D'ye ken?

Just two episodes of *Taggart* were screened during 2004 – 'Compensation' and 'Saints and Sinners'. However, in the following year ITV1 showed twelve new episodes, plus several repeats. That was more *Taggart* in one year than at any time in the show's history.

Acknowledgements

Headline Publishing Group and SMG TV Productions

Thanks to Jac Drummond and Lynn Morrison for all their invaluable assistance. Thanks to Denise Paul. And to STV for use of its photographic archive, and to Photofusion Picture Library/Alamy for Clyde Canal p. 27. We're extremely grateful to the following for their outstanding photography: Karl Attard, Charlie Crawford and Graeme Hunter; also Alan Wylie for Alex Norton, p. 166; William Allan for Kelvingrove Park, p. 97; Michael Beglan for Milngavie, p. 23 and Botanic Gardens, p. 97; Steve Cadman for Glasgow Art School, p. 100; James Crossan for Meadowside Granary, p. 98; Steve Douglas for Springburn, p. 22; Andrew Dunn for Glasgow University, p. 103; Scott Foy for Buchanan Street, p. 76; Euan Fraser for Armadillo, p. 96; Graeme for Necropolis, p. 102; John Guerrier for Kingston Bridge, p. 96; Mehran Haddadi for Glasgow Royal Concert Hall, p. 99; Victoria Hannan for Hunterian Museum, p. 103; Paul Hart for Broomielaw Bridge, p. 98; Hollowhorn for St Andrew's Bridge, Glasgow Green, p. 99; Charlie Holmes for Drumchapel, p. 23; David Jarnstrom for Central Station, p. 101; John Johnston for Maryhill, p. 22; Iraklis A. Klampanos for Kelvinbridge, p. 98; Matthew Kuhnert for Templeton Carpet Factory, p. 100; Bartosz Madejski for Gardner Street, p. 97; Laurie McGill for Glasgow Science Centre, p. 101; Dr Alan McMorran for Argyle Street Bridge, p. 77; Liliana Rodriguez for George Square, p. 102; Bob Shand for Sauchiehall Street, p. 99; John Stewart for St Enoch's Shopping Centre, p. 98; Darren Topping for Firhill, p. 99; John Williams for Barrowland, p. 102. 'No Mean City', p. 78, written by Mike Moran. Published by BMG Music Publishing Ltd. Used by permission. All rights reserved.

While every effort has been made to trace and acknowledge all copyright holders, we would like to apologise for any errors or omissions.

Thomas Quinn

A big thank you to Andrea Henry, my editor at Headline, who had the sense to ring and ask if I'd ever heard of a show called *Taggart*. Thanks also to Paul Sheehan, Eric Coulter and Graeme Gordon at SMG who opened the door to their vault and let me in; to Blythe Duff for her time and an excellent foreword; and to all those connected with the show past and present for all their assistance, particularly Alex Norton, John Michie, Colin McCredie and James Macpherson. As for Glenn Chandler and Robert Love, without them neither this book nor Britain's longest-running detective series would exist. There's been a murder, they are responsible, and I'm extremely grateful.

And thanks go to my wife, Carmen, for regularly staying up till 2 a.m. with me to help make sense of so many red herrings.

Index

(Page references in *italics* indicate a
photograph)